KV-026-526

THE CHRISTIAN APPROACH TO THE JEW

THE CHRISTIAN APPROACH TO THE JEW

BEING A REPORT OF CONFERENCES ON THE SUBJECT HELD AT BUDAPEST AND WARSAW IN APRIL 1927

LONDON
EDINBURGH HOUSE PRESS
2 EATON GATE, S.W.1
1927

Printed in Scotland
by Turnbull & Spears, Edinburgh

PREFATORY NOTE

This volume is issued under the auspices of the International Missionary Council and the Conference of Missionary Societies in Great Britain and Ireland by the Arrangements Committee for the Conferences on the Presentation of the Christian Message to the Jews, held at Budapest and Warsaw in April 1927. It contains a Report of the Conferences from the pen of the Rev. James Black, D.D., minister of United Free St. George's Church, Edinburgh.

The Findings of the Conferences are printed both in English and German, but in order to keep the volume within reasonable compass and price, the remainder is printed in English only. It should be added that very valuable papers written in German were submitted to the Conference. The writers of these have been accorded permission to make them available in German in magazine form or otherwise, and should a German edition of this Report be published, they will no doubt be included.

The Directory of Missionary Agencies has been made as complete as possible, but it does not pretend to be an exhaustive Directory.

CONTENTS

THE JEW AND THE GENTILE

A STORY OF DESPAIR AND HOPE

By Rev. JAMES BLACK, D.D.

I. The Roots of Hate

Has there been any enmity in the bleak history of human hate and misunderstanding so bitter or so unsleeping as the antagonism of Jew and Gentile ?

Many strong hates, being dignified into clan feuds, have lived for generations: this has lived for centuries. It has been the most venomous and explosive hate known to me in all human experience. It has been a *general* hate—not among one nation, but at times and in some fashion among all. It has run like a strong undercurrent through the politics, the social customs and the religion of every phase of the Christian era. In spite of all disguises and disclaimers, it is as real and as troublesome to-day in certain situations as ever it was. At times, even in what we call our age of tolerance, it bursts to the surface, as all strong undercurrents tend to do, and spreads itself in spates of havoc and folly.

In former times, the proverb that summarised man's insolent inhumanity to man was the gibe that the Jews had no dealings with the Samaritans. Since the days of the early Church—I, of course, apportion no blame—the proverb has been transmuted into the phrase that the Jews and the Christians have no dealings with each other, except indeed to slander or despoil. In that new form, the proverb at times has become a thing of unexampled hate and wickedness, wholly unguessed even in darker and ruder times. It is not straining truth to say that no age in the Christian era has been unfouled by this mutual bitterness, which runs like a " crimson thread of blood " through the tapestry of the generations.

But if this is true, I question also if there has been any enmity so unreasonable or so groundless, *once foolish prejudice and inherited hate have been bravely faced and mastered.* The links between the Jew and the Christian are so real and so beautiful, the points of contact are so spiritually deep, the " affinities " are so sure, and the debts are so mutual, that this ancient enmity is a continual source of wonderment to an enquiring mind. One feels that it is a quarrel between near relatives, literally between father and son ; and like most family feuds, the focus of bitterness has centred round irrelevant and surface things. And, as usual, the more trivial the more bitter.

II. The Church's Persecution of the Jew

On the one hand, for a hundred foolish reasons, the Christian has regarded the Jew as the prime enemy of the Cross. Jesus, the object of Christian adoration, suffered at the hands of the Jews that historic death of shame and cruelty. Because of this, with a vindictive memory, millions of Christians have cursed the race, and have libelled an innocent nation for the sins of a guilty few, and the living for the dead.

Even the Moslem, who in the age of the Crusades was the prize anathema of all Christianity, was an object of far less rancour than the powerless and landless Jew. If the Christian could fight the Moslem and his creed to the death, he treated him at least as a gentleman and an honourable foe. But there was no baiting too mean and no torture too harrowing for Christian peoples to wreak on the shivering Jews who were huddled in their midst. The system of the Ghetto, I believe, was originally a device of the Jews for their own safety, a rallying-ground where unity meant strength : but in the end it was their punishment. They were hounded as if they were a pariah people into its purlieus where they and their children lived and died like dogs. If the growing population threatened to burst the walls of the official Ghetto, then the population must be lessened!

Countless laws in countless lands enacted that no Jew could hold property or land. Apart from physical enormities of baiting and carnage, the Christian deprived the resident Jew of many political and civil rights; and as a consequence, in any time of social or religious tumult, the life of the Jew was literally at the mercy of mob-law. As a last kick, most European nations forced the Jew to wear the dress insignia of his nationality, that he might be readily known and noted—and treated as he deserved!

In all fairness, we might speculate how much this treatment of the centuries has had to do with the evolution of the modern Jew as we know him. I hear people lamenting the strangle-hold that Jewish moneyed men have on the commerce and banking of the nations. I wonder sometimes if this is not the reflex of our own acts, our indirect creation, a left-handed Nemesis of agelong treatment. By our iniquitous laws, the Jews could hold no land; and since money was the one lever that could give him a purchase on others for his skin's sake, money with its vicious usuries became the one precious thing in his outlook. To him as to no other soul in history, money was power, sometimes *life*. It may be a fact, therefore, that we have "bred into" the Jew some of the qualities whose excesses we deplore.

III. The Jew's Persecution of the Church

That is one side; the other is fully as bitter.

In their own time and opportunity the Jews have exhibited a hate and oppression as fierce as any exercised by the Church. As a matter of history, it is fair to remember that the Jew began the sorry business! The Book of Acts is annotated with records of relentless malevolence against the young Christian Church. Both as individuals and as growing societies, the Christians of early days went in daily hazard of their life. Paul had many perils by land and sea, but none so deadly as his own brethren! The roll of the martyrs makes grim reading.

Further—as I wish to be fair later on, allow me to be equally fair now—it is worth at least a passing notice that the Christian as such did not originate this orgy of aggression against the Jews. Long before the Church had any foothold or power, the Hebrew was the object of sporadic persecution from other nations, particularly from the Romans. Again and again he was driven out from prominent cities by official edicts, and chased into exile. It appears to have been an ancient game—this scourging of the Jew! The truth seems to be that there has always been something in the character or conduct of the dispersed Hebrew that has " stirred the choler " of those among whom he lived. Some would attribute this openly to the Jew's natural genius which roused the envy of outmanœuvred competitors. Others would blame his acquisitiveness, his " slimness," or his uncanny power of exploiting his fellows. I cannot but think, however, that the subtlest of all reasons lay in this—that amid every people among whom he dwelt *he remained a Jew*, always a Jew, an alien undigested element, one who could not be " assimilated " in any adequate fashion into the ordinary social and family life of the community. In the last resort, he was exclusive—exclusive in his faith, his outlook, even in his food! But the fact remains uncontested that the Jewish people were the victims of organised oppression long before the Christian Church had any standing or sway!

To balance the account finally in this appalling affair of enmity, no Jew should forget, no Christian can forget, that the Jewish people from the earliest Christian times have said unmentionable things about Jesus and His people. It would serve no good end nowadays to recall these incredible slanders. Dr Joseph Klausner, himself a Jew, has gallantly " laid these ghosts " for ever in his wonderful estimate of Jesus as the flower and boast of the Jewish race. But there can be little doubt that apart from the rowdy pagan element in Medieval Christianity—there is a good deal of Christianity that is still medieval—these disreputable slanders of our Lord converted many gentle-minded people into angry fanatics.

This then was the brutal situation until little more than a generation ago—smouldering enmity bitter and sullen on both sides, but fanned at intervals by spasmodic winds into leaping flames. This mutual enmity stood out as the world's greatest historic hate.

IV. The Changed Heart of the Church

Fortunately for the Church and the Jew alike, this impossible situation of past centuries has been changed as by magic. It has been changed, I believe, on both sides.

In point of time the change came first on the side of the Christian, perhaps because in point of need it was most demanded there. The era of missionary endeavours among the Jews was a mark and proof of the new spirit of grace in the heart of the Church. Of late days this change has become more noticeable—so noticeable indeed that it betokens a change not only of measure but of kind.

In the first place, the conscience of the Church has been deeply stirred in regard to its duty to this scattered race who stand in the world as a miracle of God's providence. Too long have we left the Jew to himself as some one almost past reclaiming. Perhaps our manhood and our resources were too fully engaged in the overwhelming problem of the heathen, a problem that at one time seemed to offer a more immediate and proportionate reward to work and money. It used to be said as a cheap gibe that it took too much time and cash to convert a Jew! But the Church has been learning in late days that it cannot measure any adequate work for Christ by its immediate returns, or by its ease of accomplishment, or by the magic of numbers, as one counts sheep. In a matter of high policy for the welfare of Christianity, it may be as rewarding to win fifteen millions of Jews living in the heart of Christianity and subtly colouring its culture and ideals, as to win thirty millions who live outside it.

In the second place, Christians at last have gained the insight and the courage to condemn the devil's spirit of persecution and ostracism. In my own mind, nothing has more helped the Christian outlook for work among thinking Jews than the open and frank repentance of the Churches for all ancient wrong and outrage. This was an acknowledgment of sin that was long overdue. The dragging years of agony inflicted on this outcast people are beyond any attempt at justification or even mitigation. It is only the tears of a cleansing repentance that can ever wipe out the wrongs of the centuries from the savage memory of this martyred race.

It is right, therefore, that our first approach to the Jew should be by the shadowed way of penitence and shame. We must shoulder the sins of our fathers. We must even, if need be, shoulder the sins of many of our brethren in other lands who still cast slanting eyes on the troublesome Jew.

As a third consideration, Christians are re-seeing the forgotten fact that Jesus was a Jew, sprung from Jewish stock and reared in the Jewish environment and faith. Some people shrink from speaking of our Lord in this plain fashion. But why should any one be blind to the fact that in God's good providence Jesus was born and bred among the Hebrew race and lived amid Hebrew inheritances? The implications of this fact are plain and commanding for any thinking Christian—the Jews are *His brethren, His kinsmen, His "ain folk."* He loved them; He worked for them; He longed to win them; He died by them and for them. Could there be a more splendid appeal or a greater drive in our hearts than this? I think it is a matter of fine promise that good people speak of the Jews less as Christ's murderers and more as Christ's brethren!

Still further, the Church at last is facing the one inescapable argument for all Jewish work of reconciliation—that it is based not on policy or need or even love, good though these may be, but on the definite command of the Lord. This is the final thing to say—that it is *the Lord's will* that His own people, the lost sheep of the House of Israel, should be saved. When we think of this passion of His heart, we cannot but say that all the brutal work of past days which alienated the Hebrews from Jesus and caused them to spit at that holy name, must have drawn tears from the angels ! Persecution, which usually defeats its own purpose, has only hardened Jewry like a flint against the Christian religion : and the foolish zeal for the cross that led people to curse and taunt the Jew, has spelt the defeat, or at least the delay, of Christ's dream.

And lastly, from the Church's point of view, the Jew, as never before, has been discovered to be reachable—we believe, gloriously reachable. There are possibilities of extended work to-day that were undreamt of in past times. Jewry is finally outside the Ghetto : and its people are open to all reasonable influence. It will be a tragedy if they accept Christian civilisation without its Christ.

V. A New Day in Jewry

But if these healthy changes have taken place in the mind and heart of the Christian, there have been balancing changes, as unexpected and as promising, on the side of the Jew. Naturally, since the main problem lay in the closed mind of the Hebrew, the greatest note of hope for the future lies here. We believe that if Christians could be brought to realise all that these changes portend, there would be a new passion and a new sacrifice for Jewish Evangelisation. It is in this hope that we broadcast our report of these Conferences with so much expectancy and assurance.

We ask all Christian Churches, agencies, and people to consider very prayerfully the opportunities presented in the following facts which are in public evidence everywhere.

1. The Ghetto and all the deplorable things it represented are things of the past. The walls of Jericho have fallen. Praise God!

This means an era of another and more hopeful dispersion of the Jews. In a new liberation that is not only political but also mental and spiritual, they are mixing freely on equal terms with Christians and assuming their long-denied birthright of citizenship; and the closed mind, which was the product of the fixed unchanging life of the Ghetto itself, is quickly passing. In this modern dispersion, they are thinking and reading freely—a matter of mingled promise and danger. But the point is, for their own good or ill, *they are out in the open.* With a few grave exceptions, they are being treated with a natural friendliness that must be disarming for many of their ancient hostilities. All evidence shows that they are enquiring, constantly enquiring. This is Christ's great chance.

2. The miracle of the dismantled Ghetto—an indirect result of the European war which broke so many despotisms—means that the world of Jewry, once so solid, is now fluid.

Literally, as well as figuratively, the Jews are "on the move." In Central and Eastern Europe, where they are most populous, the upheaval of war produced some amazing transformations. Ancient traditions toppled with the empires that buttressed them. The Jews, who were No Man's People, were called out into "No Man's Land," and stood shoulder to shoulder on equal terms and in equal adventure with the men of the pike and the gun. They took part in political and social revolutions, and helped to carve out new empires. With the Gilbertian changing of boundaries and frontiers, they went to sleep in one nation and woke in the morning to find themselves in another.

Thereafter, during the plastic post-war years, they have migrated in larger numbers than at any time since they tramped into captivity to Babylon, or since they were outlawed from the territories of the Spanish empire. This migration from state to state, especially when contrasted with the stagnation of generations, has meant not only a change of environment but a change of mind. We can hardly comprehend what these kaleidoscopic transformations have meant for the younger Jews.

The stiff unbending life of former days, set in the rigid framework of an enclosed Ghetto, is gone. Formerly, that Ghetto shut its people off from any real opportunity of outside cultural influences. For one thing, they were held in the grip of precise Talmudic teaching; and their natural loyalty to their own religion was stiffened by an intense corporate resistance to the unfriendly world that either slandered or shunned them. It was only by massed loyalty to their race and faith that they could resist the push of an environment that threatened to crush them. And one must admit that Jewry's fidelity to its religion has been one of the seven wonders of the world.

The fall of the Ghetto has meant the end of this cloistral seclusion. They are out in the open, living the normal life of other people, and joining in the free market of formative ideas. Needless to say, there lie in this some splendid possibilities and many perils, for the change means not only political, but *spiritual* enfranchisement. So far as their ancient faith is concerned, they have embarked on a spiritual adventure.

3. A direct outcome of this widespread political and social liberation is that the Jews have come into closer touch with modern scientific ideas. For young eager minds the passage from the obscurantism of Talmudic teaching to the free discussion of modern enquiry must have been an amazing experience. It is little wonder that it has proved disturbing and unbalancing. Wise people will be chary of laying too much stress on the fact that many of the younger enfranchised Jews have cast aside religious beliefs and sanctions, and have embraced plain revolutionism in religion and politics. In many ways this is only the natural swing of the pendulum; after years of prison, it is hard to distinguish between liberty and licence! We cannot judge average Jewish mentality in relation to modern

problems and opportunities from the excesses of some Jews of our day, who have no political heredity and no consolidating traditions behind them. Good people will be sympathetic with this strangely disturbing liberation with its wide horizons that contrast so startlingly with the foreclosed outlook of the Ghetto.

It must be admitted, none the less, that the new wine has been distilled into a revolutionary ferment. Religion and many of our accepted political theories have been discarded : and thousands of eager young Jews have found a substitute religion in sweeping forms of socialistic idealism and universal brotherhood.

4. As a natural result of this upheaval, there has been a wide departure from the synagogues. Leaders of Judaism have complained bitterly of a desertion of worship and a disregard of authority. This is not a matter for any rejoicing on our part. It will be a bitter day if good Jews are only converted into bad Jews ! There is no finer type of citizen than a strict Jew who loves God's will, obeys His commandments, and is under the sanctions and inhibitions of a great religion. But we have to face facts; and one alarming fact to-day seems to be the drift from the synagogue and a lapse from Judaism as an outworn creed, no longer able to satisfy the enquiring Hebrew youth amid the puzzles and problems of modern thought.

Our only source of congratulation may be that though this lapse should prove immediately disturbing for religion and morals in our time, it may ultimately present a great chance for the Gospel of Jesus among His own brethren. If this were so—we should need to jump at once to the opportunity !—it might turn disaster into triumph. At present, we must realise that the new situation offers a challenge and an opportunity to the Church of our Lord. We have no longer a stagnant, but a moving people ; and happily, in spite of some obnoxious forms of anti-semitic feeling, we have a younger race that is unacquainted with persecution except by hearsay, a race therefore with less bias and prejudice, and more open to impression and friendly dealing.

It has been a generation of amazing changes for the Jew—a people, long cooped up in prison and in the bonds of a stereotyped system, now free and moving and enquiring; a people who have seen the shallowness of their faith and, for want of a better, are now turning to materialism, agnosticism or communism; and finally, a people who offer a new chance for the traduced Saviour of their race.

VI. The Preparation for the Conferences

It was this situation, with its possible expansions for weal or woe, that made the Conferences at Budapest and Warsaw imperative.

Big work by many Churches and in many lands has been undertaken for the Jew. But so much of that work, while finely done and greatly blessed, was sporadic, unrelated, if not sometimes competitive and divisive. There was a real need for all active agencies to correlate results, compare methods, exchange experiences, devise new and more effective means, and form better links of co-operation. This does not reflect on the quality of the work that was done in the past. Churches, Societies, and small groups of men and women have given themselves and their resources in fine generosity on behalf of the Jews. But they have been comparatively scant in numbers, and have often lacked vision and leadership. And, on the whole, they have ploughed lonely furrows.

A big problem like this needs the whole Church, *the whole Church alive*. If the Conferences do nothing else than bring the problem in its full scope before the Christian public, showing its urgency, its possibilities, and its dangers, and if they only startle the Church to see the uniqueness of the occasion, they will not have failed of their purpose. But mere wonder will do nothing. Wonder must be harnessed, and then hitched into the shafts as *work*!

In face of this new situation in the world of Jewry, the majority of the Societies in Protestant Christianity met together, by official delegates, in April 1927 at Budapest in Hungary and Warsaw in Poland. With Dr John R. Mott of the United States of America as chairman, and Dr Macdonald Webster of Edinburgh as secretary, there were representatives from Europe, Asia, Africa and America—a real world-conference, the first that had ever been held regarding Jewish Evangelisation. The general subject of discussion was the chief of all topics—" The Christian Message to the Jews."

The Conferences were exceedingly happy in their chairman, for amid the natural differences of language, outlook and temperament that marked such a cosmopolitan gathering, Dr Mott was courtesy, fairness and clearness personified. He is by nature and training a prince among chairmen. I think that every delegate would acknowledge most gratefully that he received a fair hearing for himself and his views, amid a sympathetic brotherhood.

For the immense spade-work—not only of months, but of years—which enabled the Conferences to be as successful as they were, the credit lies with Dr Macdonald Webster and his staff. He himself had been a distinguished missionary among the Jews of Europe for many years, and it has always been his dream to arrange such Conferences as these in order that Jewish work might be co-ordinated and inspired. I am sure that he must have had signal joy in the results of his efforts.

Some of this preliminary spade-work for the Conferences is worth recalling. Eighteen months before the meeting a detailed questionnaire was prepared, dealing exhaustively with every aspect of Jewish Evangelisation. Copies of this document were sent over the world to approved missionaries and Church workers of many denominations. When the replies were received, representing the authoritative experience of first-class workers in all types of service, a digest of the information was skilfully drafted, and when published was distributed to every delegate. The summary of this questionnaire is so valuable that it is printed in the Appendix to this Report.

Mention should be made of another preliminary pamphlet for which Dr Macdonald Webster's staff is also responsible. Some noted men—masters in their own subject—were "roped in" to write articles on important aspects of the Jewish question. These articles were published and distributed to the delegates. Some of these papers were so outstanding and so deserving of a larger audience that a selection from them is also published in the Appendix.

The financing of such a large undertaking, with delegates from all parts of the world—there were roughly one hundred delegates both at Budapest and Warsaw—was only made possible by the generosity of the International Missionary Council, of which Dr Mott is chairman. The Council most willingly supplemented the contributions of the individual Societies, and removed any danger of possible financial stringency. I am sure that the individual Churches and Societies whose delegates were present, extend to the Council their sincere thanks.

Incidentally also, it was a great gain that these Conferences took place under the captaincy of the International Missionary Council. I question if any other body could have united the scattered elements of Jewish Christian service in so universal a sweep and with such harmony. The Conferences met under the advantage of being summoned by an organisation that is itself world-wide in its constitution. Most of all, it was enriched by the accumulated experience of the Council and of Dr Mott, its chairman.

VII. The Work of the Conference

"It would have been a collective crime not to have come together to revise our thought and action in face of the new situation throughout the Jewish world."

This telling sentence from the opening speech of the Chairman summarises the objects of the Conferences. The problem was immediately tackled. For convenience, and to avoid sporadic discussion and needless overlapping, the general topic was divided into the following sub-sections—evangelisation and message, methods of work (medical, industrial, community centres, etc.), literature, the training, equipment and care of workers, special work among women, the occupation of the field, the growth and maintenance of spiritual power, and co-operation. The Conference had three daily sessions—morning, afternoon, and evening ; and the delegates, keen on their work, attended with fine fidelity.

" Plenary Sessions " of the Conference were first of all held. Here the various sub-sections were opened out swiftly and suggestively by chosen speakers who gave the results of collated experience. These speeches were followed by general discussion. This discussion never flagged, and was maintained at a high level of interest and Christian foresight and policy.

The difficulties of language were finely overcome by a band of admirable translators, who gave a clear digest of every speech—indeed of each question and interjected remark—in either English or German according to need. The average in each language was fairly even, with perhaps a slight preponderance of German over English at Budapest, and a proportionate reversal of this at Warsaw. No speech was allowed to exceed five minutes, with the exception of the leader who introduced each special topic ; and, as Mr Basil Mathews remarked, " Those who were more succinct were more popular."

Mr Mathews, whom I have just quoted, has a fine experience of the difficulties of this type of international gathering. I quote further from a lively account of the Budapest Conference, which he has kindly sent me. " The processes of translation were salutary from every point of view. They emphasised the need for patient sympathetic intellectual effort, if cultural, national and linguistic differences are to be overcome, and understanding is to be achieved. They gave us time to think in between speeches ; and to think twice before speaking often reveals the needlessness of what one was going to say. And more than once a translation in the midst of a discussion, where differences were sharp and deep, and where the speakers were developing more heat than light, the quiet pause while the speech was being delivered in another language gave men the chance to regain perspective and their sense of humour. A considerable number of the delegates had clearly never taken part in a fully international discussion, and the processes of interchange through the translation were only one element in an educational process of international interpretation that is salutary to us all. It became increasingly clear that differences of outlook were not along national frontiers but across them ; and above all that, beneath all the differences, lay unexpectedly rich abundant and fertile soil of unity."

The real stress of the Conference began after the Plenary Sessions had done their preparatory work of ploughing and harrowing, with the soil well loosened out. Instructed and toned by the general discussions, the delegates were allotted in fairly equal numbers to various " Findings Committees." Each had its own subject to tackle, and retired for some sessions to a private room, like a dog in a corner gnawing a meaty bone !

The duty of a Findings Committee was very outspokenly, but very tactfully defined by our imperturbable Chairman. Plainly, its duty was to *find* something—something worth finding ! It would do nobody any good to rake up obvious, ancient and tattered things lying at our feet. It was useless to find things that had never been lost—things better lost—things which no sensible man ever wanted to find ! Guidance for the world from God's heart—that was our search. None the less, one should not be coward enough to shirk a platitude, just because it was true. If it was true, did it need to be said ? Did it need to be said, perhaps, again and again, until it edged itself into the obtuse conscience of mankind ? If so, *how* should it be said ? Each committee was urged to be adventurous, daring and candid, and yet never overstepping either truth or need.

I should like my readers, therefore, to understand that the Findings published in this book have been hammered out day after day by a body of earnest and informed men and women, and were passed afterwards, in minute discussion, by the whole Conference. We print them in this volume because we believe in their solid and permanent value. They represent the considered judgment of almost two hundred knowledgeable men and women, most of them people with a lifelong experience of their subject and area. If there seems to be any small repetition of phrase or idea in the results of the two Conferences, I ask you to believe that we have left that repetition uncensored in order that it may bring its *double message* to the Christian conscience and heart. If there is anything that appears obvious, we have left it unpruned because it was so obvious that people have failed to see it ! If there is anything on which everybody seems agreed, we print it because there is nothing so dangerous to the Church, or so neglected by the Church, as the things on which we are all agreed. As Coleridge remarks, " Our greatest mission is to rescue admitted truths from the neglect caused by their admission."

But we believe that these are real " *findings* " in the best sense of the idea. We asked the blessing of God on these Conferences, and we believe that His Spirit was with us. In that belief, we send out our results in the faith that they will give light and direction to all good work for the people of Jesus. I shall not speak of these Findings in any detail. I think they can speak for themselves. But I cannot refrain from saying a word about the atmosphere in which they were born. The delegates felt that they were living in a big day of opportunity, where there were open doors and sunlight. Men and women, like the returning apostles of our Lord, told of the great things God had done for them, and they hailed this means of informing and stirring the Church regarding its great inheritance of duty and privilege.

I close this somewhat cursory introduction by a reference to what was the most notable element of hope to my own heart. An unbiassed reader might well discount anything I have said, if he pictures this Conference as a gathering of enthusiastic Gentiles, blandly deceived by hearsay, and credulous enough to confuse hopes with facts. For myself, I should have distrusted any pronouncement made by a Gentile Conference regarding the inner life of that secret folk, the Jews. But a large proportion of the delegates was Jewish-Christian—people born and reared in Hebrew traditions, who have glorified their ancient faith by glorifying the Messiah. It was a gladdening thing to see the number and the quality of these Hebrew-Christian evangelists. In the last resort, with adequate training, the Jews will make the best apostles to the Jews. They can tell—as they did tell at the Conference—what Jesus Messiah has meant to their own souls. And from my knowledge of these men I look forward with great hope and confidence to the day when the Hebrew-Christians will lead in the great venture of Jesus for His own folk.

Meanwhile, the Conferences solemnly prayed for the full blessing of God upon the Hebrew-Christian Alliance.

I take this public opportunity in the name of the two Conferences to thank the Cities of Budapest and Warsaw—is it possible to thank a city ?—for their wonderful courtesy and kindness to the delegates during our happy stay within their borders. We thank also the local Committees in each city for their meticulous arrangements for our welfare and for unfailing kindness to many inexperienced travellers. And finally, not least, we thank the Scottish Mission in Budapest and the Church House of the Evangelical Lutheran Church of Warsaw for the hospitality of their halls for our numerous meetings, and for the guidance of their superintendents and workers.

THE FINDINGS OF THE BUDAPEST CONFERENCE

I. Evangelisation and Message

I. While this Conference recognises the responsibility of every Church and of individual Christians to the Jews dwelling in their neighbourhood, there is also an urgent and growing need for special evangelisation among the Jews of the world. This work should be conducted directly, and the agents should be specially trained. The need and urgency of the work should be laid impressively on the heart of the whole Church of Christ.

We mention the following as reasons for this special evangelisation :—

(*a*) The authority of Scripture, and the love of Jesus for His own race.
(*b*) The peculiar life and environment of the Jews.
(*c*) Their spiritual mentality and capacity.
(*d*) The present unique opportunities through the disruption of their ancient faith.
(*e*) The evidences of a ready welcome in wide areas.
(*f*) The spiritual gain which Jewish zeal would bring to the Christian Church.

We urge Christians everywhere to repentance for prejudice and persecution which unfortunately are not yet things of the past, and in some countries are identified with professedly Christian organisations. We believe that all unchristian treatment of the Jew and all race-prejudice are great stumbling-blocks to the acceptance of the Christian message.

II. Our message to the Jews is the love of God revealed in Jesus Christ, crucified, risen, glorified, the fulfilment of the law and the true Messiah. He is the incarnate Word, the Redeemer of the world, the Saviour from sin, who is bringing Israel to her destiny—viz., to become a blessing to all humanity.

This message should be presented with humility and love and with self-sacrificing service, so that the Jews may be awakened from the mere expectancy of a Messiah or a dependence on self-righteousness to true repentance and confession of sin, praying for regeneration, receiving pardon through the sacrifice of the Lord Jesus, and becoming His sincere disciples.

III. In the religion of Israel there are ideas of culture and principles of morality which are not to be found in other non-Christian religions. The Jew and the Christian have in common the Old Testament which is the vehicle of God's revelation to mankind, a heritage not enjoyed by other non-Christian religions. The Jew, moreover, has a unique consciousness of his role in the purpose of God for the salvation of the world.

Therefore, in approaching the Jewish religion, in distinction from other non-Christian religions, regard should be paid to this religious heritage of Israel. The difference in the religious approach between the followers of other non-Christian religions and of Judaism is that the one is led to God through Jesus Christ, while the Jew is led to Jesus Christ through his previous knowledge of God, however incomplete.

IV. Considering the vast extent of the Jewish Mission field and the different types of Jews amongst whom we are called to labour, we believe that the methods employed in our work should be made specially suitable for various localities, and for varied grades of culture. There is no one stereotyped method applicable to all circumstances. This refers also to the presentation of the message. Any particular method which needlessly awakens the opposition of the Jews should be avoided and discouraged.

V. We call attention to the fact that baptism, prematurely performed, often makes the baptised Jew a stumbling-block to other Jews, and a reproach to the Mission and to the Church.

When a Jew applies for baptism, the missionary should do his utmost to test his profession and observe his life, lest there be any ulterior motives in his mind.

The aim of missions is not to "make propaganda," but to win souls for Christ and lead them to holy living. The missionary ought, therefore, to show special caution in admitting for baptism those for whom there is no community of Christian people prepared to receive the converts and give them the necessary spiritual help and guidance. A period of wise and careful instruction should precede baptism, and, where possible, an accurate register of baptisms should be kept.

II. Christian Education

I. It is the duty of the members of the Christian Church as the servants of the Christ, who gathered the little ones of Israel into His arms and blessed them, to endeavour to win the hearts of the youth of Israel to-day to that Saviour, who is theirs by every right. To this end schools and hostels should be maintained or started wherever there is still the possibility of doing so. For this purpose a survey of the field, occupied and unoccupied, is urgently needed.

The aims of such schools must be, firstly, the creation of a Christian atmosphere in the school, and the guiding of the young mind toward the person of Christ, and secondly, the provision of the best secular education possible. Such schools will provide the necessary education for the children of converts and of Jews who desire a Christian or higher moral training for their children. They will be clear evidence of Christian love in places where no adequate provision for education exists, or where anti-semitic influence makes the public schools almost intolerable to the Jew. Further, they will help to save the youth of Israel from the indifference or hostility to religion which rob them of life's highest values, and make them a menace to society.

II. The expenditure of time and money on such schools is justified by the results. The direct results are :—(*a*) The baptism of pupils, with the consent of their parents, on reaching the age at which the law of the land allows a change of religion; (*b*) the large number of secret followers of Christ produced by such schools. The indirect results are :—(*a*) The friendlier attitude towards Christianity, and the greater respect for the Mission induced by contract with Christian teaching and real Christian life and love; (*b*) the missionary opportunities thereby created.

III. Certain essentials should be kept in mind :—

(*a*) The school should compare favourably with schools of a similar type in the respective countries. Hence the staff must be fully qualified, the buildings and equipment up to date, and the curriculum of the highest standard.

(*b*) The staff should consist wholly, as far as possible, of those whose desire it is by teaching and life to lead the children to Christ.

(*c*) There must be liberty to give full and unrestricted teaching of the New Testament and Christian truths, and sufficient teachers who specialise in the presentation of Christian truth to Jewish children.

(*d*) The course of instruction provided must be such as to retain the pupils as long as possible under Christian influence.

(*e*) Nothing should be done which would tend to alienate the pupils from their own people, and definite instruction might well be given in Jewish history, and, where desired by the parents, in the Hebrew language.

(*f*) Provision must be made and the requisite teachers set apart for keeping in touch with the children after leaving school by means of clubs, classes and correspondence, and, where necessary, by the provision of hostels for those who have professed their faith in Christ.

(*g*) In view of the future of the boys and girls there

should be as a rule schools for both sexes in any given Mission.

(*h*) The work in the schools should be followed up in the children's homes by the teachers and specially appointed visitors.

IV. There are certain problems which will need to be grappled with :—

(*a*) The attitude of Governments to Mission schools.

(*b*) The state of public opinion in some countries on the subject of early marriage and the withdrawal from school at an early age of the pupils.

(*c*) The high cost of maintenance of Mission schools in those lands where the standard of education is highest or the standard of life very low.

V. This does not exhaust the duty of the Christian Church to the children and young people of Jewry. Churches and Missions should endeavour to attract and influence the Jewish youth in their neighbourhood by such means as play centres, educational and physical training classes, summer camps, vacation Bible schools, etc., each and all being coupled with very definite Christian teaching, at which the attendance is wholly voluntary.

VI. It is most desirable that all Christian movements among the youth of both sexes, such as the Student Christian Movement, Y.M.C.A., Y.W.C.A., Boy Scouts, Girl Guides, Boys' and Girls' Brigades, etc., should be encouraged to include the Jewish youth in their purview and activities.

III. Medical Missions, Philanthropy and Community Centres

I. With regard to Medical Mission work :—

1. The obligation to care for the bodies as well as for the souls of men is a positive principle inherent in the Christian faith, illustrated and enforced by the example and practice of Christ.

2. This principle lays an obligation upon Christian Missions to provide, as far as their means allow, for the needs in question.

3. Where medical missionary institutions are established, great and equal emphasis should be placed upon the efficiency of staff and equipment from both the medical and missionary standpoints. Efficiency from both of these standpoints requires that, at least in every institution of considerable size, the missionary service of the doctors and nurses should be supplemented by those of other agents specially devoted to evangelistic work.

4. All patients should be invited to attend religious services at which the message of the Gospel is presented. Under some circumstances it may be wise to make attendance a condition of admittance to the hospital, but this cannot be insisted upon under all circumstances.

5. All patients, able to do so, should pay in whole or in part for the medical service rendered, and also for food and other expenses incurred on their behalf. Patients without the means to pay should receive the best services that the institution can give without any charges being made for the same.

6. Public dispensaries, the services of qualified midwives, district work by nurses, may be considered as normal auxiliaries to hospitals and should be carried on where need for the same exists. These services often prove of great benefit and value in areas where an hospital cannot be placed. Findings made above with regard to payment apply to those receiving the services of these auxiliaries.

7. The results of medical work are many and encouraging.

II. With regard to Homes :—

1. For Enquirers :—Homes for enquirers are of great value. They should be established and controlled by the respective Mission Board or Society.

2. For Baptised Converts :—Homes for baptised converts are also of great value, but current considerations, relating to cost of upkeep and to industrial conditions in

general, render impracticable the establishment and conduct of such homes in sufficient numbers except upon an interdenominational or international basis. The International Hebrew Christian Alliance, on account of the personal history and experience of its members, is specially fitted for the work of establishing and conducting such homes.

III. With regard to Community Centres:—In certain special areas in North America, with an admixture of population representing several races and religious faiths, the Christian Community Centre has been employed with distinct and encouraging results.

IV. Other Forms of Philanthropy:—Other forms of philanthropy, such as homes or other provision for the aged or for orphans, rest upon the general principles of Christian benevolence, and are desirable where the means of the Mission permit of the provision of the same. Recipients of relief for temporary distress should, when physically able, be urged to return some service for the same.

IV. Christian Literature

I. There exists an extensive literature, which, although written without special reference to Jewish national or religious conditions, may be used to awaken among Jews an understanding of Christianity. It is recommended that a selection of the best of such literature be drawn up in furtherance of the approach to educated Jewry.

II. Of literature, written specially for Jews, some is out of date; some has been weakened in its influence by an extreme polemic character or a disputable apologetic—elements not to be wholly set aside, but to be mellowed by the spirit of comprehending sympathy; some has a permanent value because of its proclamation of eternal verities. It is recommended that the Catalogue, begun by the late Dr Strack, and amplified by Canon Lukyn Williams, be published.

III. For the production of new literature, the following recommendations are made :—

(*a*) New literature is desirable for the Jews of these categories—(1) Orthodox, (2) Reformed, (3) Progressive, with special provision for the women in each class.

(*b*) Special literature is required for materialistic Jews, for school children, and for students.

(*c*) Regard should be given to the cultural conditions and to the languages spoken in the countries in which the Jews reside.

IV. New works on the following subjects are particularly needed :—

The Beginnings of Christianity, including the Life of Christ ; Epochs of Church History ; Studies on Christian Doctrine and Ethics ; Biographies, especially of celebrated Jewish converts ; Devotional Works, including Prayers and Hymn-books, in polyglot or other forms.

The above may be in book or pamphlet form, written, when necessary, in popular style, and illustrated.

V. Literature about the Jews for Christians :—The Conference recommends that a central organisation be established to survey literature intended to give Christians a right conception of the Jews and of their responsibilities to them, and urges the great need of issuing new, up to date and inexpensive literature on the Jews.

VI. Contact with Missionaries :—The Conference recommends that missionaries working among Jews be supplied through their Societies with information regarding literature which might prove useful to them in their several spheres. To this end a bureau, with a Central Secretary, should be established for the exchange and circulation of such literature.

VII. Co-operation :—It will prove impossible to meet the above requirements with economy and efficiency unless there is co-operation. Such co-operation should cover—

(*a*) Survey of the fields and their needs from the standpoint of literature supply.

(*b*) Selection of suitable authors and translators.

(*c*) Contact with publishing houses of repute to secure the issue of literature required.

(*d*) Organisation of methods of distribution through the trade, through mission workers, colporteurs and Bible-women.

We recommend the establishment under the International Missionary Council of a central co-ordinating office, which must be in contract with (*a*) the principal intellectual and academic centres whose resources could be usefully secured for the creation of the requisite literature, and (*b*) the various Christian organisations working among Jews.

We request the International Missionary Council to appoint four committees, the work of which should be co-ordinated by a Central Secretary. These four committees should represent work in Eastern Europe, Central Europe, Great Britain and North America. The Central Secretary should be appointed by the International Missionary Council.

VIII. Finance :—A fund will be required to provide the expenses of the Secretary, even if a voluntary worker can be found, and to meet as necessary the cost of authorship, publication and distribution. Such a fund cannot well be established by means of a general appeal, or by contributions from Christian agencies working among Jews. It might rather be considered whether friends interested would contribute to a capital fund in order to initiate the work and carry it over the experimental period, in the hope that ultimately the organisation may be paid for out of profits from sales.

V. Occupation of the Field

I. In view of far-reaching changes taking place in Jewry, especially since the War, namely, the development of a new attitude on the part of Jews towards Judaism itself, and of a more sympathetic interest in Christianity, particularly in the Person of Jesus, we urge on the Christian Church a study of Jewish needs and longings, both spiritual and intellectual. The above attitude opens a new door for Christlike service, and affords a large opportunity of presenting Christ in all His significance to His own race.

A race numbering over fifteen millions, widely scattered, keen, resourceful and capable of furnishing powerful reinforcements for the spread of the Gospel, must not be neglected. The present situation is a clear and urgent call to the Church to enter and occupy effectively those almost neglected areas where the largest Jewish populations are to be found, *e.g.*, Eastern Europe, including Russia, and the larger cities of North America.

The adoption of a sound policy of occupation and of maturely considered methods of work and administration is of prime importance. For the present, any new forces should be utilised to bring institutions at strategic centres to high efficiency in order that their influence may have a wider outreach.

II. Recognising that the Jewish field has not received careful and comprehensive study, we urge the International Missionary Council—

(*a*) To undertake such a survey of the Jewish field as has been made of the Moslem world.

(*b*) Subsequently to take counsel with Christian agencies able to undertake an advanced work for the Jews, so that as far as possible particular areas may be assigned to bodies equipped to occupy those areas, that overlapping and unseemly rivalry may be eliminated, and thus the whole field be more adequately occupied.

III. As a result of the passing of the Ghetto and of the increasingly great share taken by Jews in the whole life of the modern world, millions of Jews are now living in the midst of Christian communities, and under the shadow of Christian Churches. These Jews represent various elements, for the most part outside the range of existing Jewish missions, and they must remain unevangelised unless the local churches themselves undertake this work.

This situation is a distinct call of God to all churches having Jews in their parishes and to home missionary agencies to include them in their ministry.

IV. In view of the fact that, wherever no bar exists against them, Jewish students are to be found in Universities and Colleges in numbers out of all proportion to the number of Jews in the population; in view also of the great influence of these students in the State, and in the professions in after life, we urge that the leaders of all Student Christian Movements should include Jewish students in their purview, and that Christian students should be urged to cultivate friendly relations with Jewish as well as other non-Christian students.

V. Believing that the time has come for Christian Churches to put on record their attitude towards the Jewish people, we, as a Conference of Christian workers, deplore the long record of injustice to and ill-usage of Jews on the part of nominally Christian people. We declare such injustice and ill-usage to be a violation of the teaching and Spirit of Christ; we call upon Churches and Christians everywhere to oppose all such injustice and ill-usage, and to express to Jews by word and act the Spirit of Jesus Christ our Lord, their Saviour and ours.

We would not separate our Jewish friends from their past or rob them of that heritage which is ours as well as theirs, but we are convinced that in acceptance of Christ by their people their highest welfare will be secured. We express, moreover, the wish and the hope that, through a common allegiance to Christ, as Lord and Saviour, a rapprochement between Christians and Jews may be secured by means of which we may go forward unitedly to seek the redemption of humanity, and the establishment upon earth of the Kingdom of God.

Addendum on Palestine

Palestine contains 1 per cent. of the Jewish population of the world; yet, if we take mere numbers into account, it draws to itself 12 per cent. of the missionary man-power. The fact is that, though there are many "missions," there are but few "missionaries" in the sense of men qualified for direct and profitable contact with the Palestinian Jew.

The "over-occupation" problem turns on Jerusalem rather than on Palestine as a whole. The fact that Jerusalem is the Holy City makes it deserving of our special care; but it equally makes it essential to eliminate or denounce much that is unwise and even unworthy in the use that is made of the appeal from the Holy City.

The real strategic importance of Palestine does not turn on the number or probable increase of the Jewish population, but on the new culturally dynamic elements of Judaism which are now pouring into Palestine in the persons of outstanding leaders in Jewish literature, art, scholarship, thought and journalism. These, so far, have not shown themselves hostile to Christianity, but rather the reverse. It is among such classes that there has appeared conspicuously the tendency to revise the Jewish attitude toward Jesus.

It is now clearly within our power in Palestine to sweeten the atmosphere in the areas of Christian-Jewish contacts, and to induce a heightened respect for Christianity. But if matters continue as they now are, with the best and most influential elements in modern Judaism faced by (to say the least) inadequate and sometimes unworthy Christian representation, there must follow an increased contempt for Christianity among just those people whose opinion we should be at most pains to influence.

Attention should be drawn to the artificial conditions in Palestine. The country is, so to speak, a "museum" of ecclesiastical, cultural and political types, ranging from the seventh to the twenty-first centuries. None of these is leading its natural life in its natural surroundings, but is primarily concerned in showing itself at its best and most characteristic in this source of the Christian or the Jewish faith. Thus we have types, good or bad, but presumably representative of ancient or modern Judaism or Jewish civilisation, and of every form of Christianity, ancient and modern, reformed and unreformed.

We shall foster the cause and credit of Christianity in Palestine not by an increase in the number of workers whose only qualification is their responsiveness to the sentimental appeal of the Holy Land, but by the efforts of the Churches and Societies in doing all that is in their power to raise the efficiency of the existing institutions in their charge, and by scrupulous care in the choice of those who have to play the important rôle of Christian delegates in the Holy Land. Advance can only come by showing forth in this supreme centre of our Faith the worthiest types of Christian devotion, thought and scholarship.

VI. Training and Welfare of Workers

I. Missionary Societies ought to assure themselves that all candidates for the mission field possess real Christian experience and character.

II. Missionary leaders ought to be equipped with a biblical, theological and general education which is up to the standard required for the ordinary ministry of the Church, together with an education in Jewish subjects which will enable them to bring the Gospel effectively before all kinds of Jews. Other workers, including colporteurs, should receive such training as may be necessary for the efficient discharge of the duties assigned to them.

III. Missionary Societies, acting in fellowship, ought to strengthen institutions such as the Institutum Judaicum Delitzschianum, Leipzig, which exist to supply an adequate Jewish learning, and, if and when the necessity arises, be prepared to establish similar institutions in other parts of the world which should, as far as possible, be always associated with Universities.

IV. If the Missions are to get the type of worker which is required, the Churches must show a better understanding and a higher appreciation both of the work and the workers, and use all available means to bring the claims of the Mission before their numbers.

(*a*) It is of special importance that these claims should be brought before theological and other students in every possible way, but especially through such organisations as the World Student Christian Federation and its affiliated national movements.

(*b*) The Mission Boards, on their part, must also give special attention to the winning of their most promising converts for the work, and organisations representing Hebrew Christians should be invited to co-operate in this effort.

V. Missionary leaders and workers ought to receive adequate remuneration, and satisfactory arrangements should be made for furlough, further opportunities for study, and provision for sickness and old age.

VII. Spiritual Power

I. The Conference has met under a deep sense of the greatness of its resources in God through Christ. It rejoices that in the Word made Flesh there dwells all the fullness of the Godhead bodily, and that all the resources necessary for the work of His Kingdom are made available through His indwelling Spirit. The members of the Conference would accordingly seek from Him a fresh experience of His love in Jesus Christ and of the mighty working of His Spirit, and would humbly dedicate themselves anew to the service of the Gospel.

II. Believing that the work of Jewish Evangelisation requires the highest type of spiritual instrument for its effective discharge, and that the deepening of the spiritual life of the worker is of supreme importance, the Conference would urge that the work of each Mission and station be so arranged as to afford to the workers more adequate opportunities for regular Bible study, prayer and Christian fellowship, and is convinced that, even if the activities of a Mission are thereby reduced, those activities will be so

greatly enhanced in quality that the work as a whole will be immeasurably strengthened.

III. Believing that the spiritual power of the missionaries must to a large extent depend on the spiritual life of the home constituency, the members of the Conference would invite that constituency to join with them in a deeper penitence for past failure, in a fuller surrender to the influences of the Holy Spirit, and in a new search into the rich mine of spiritual resources provided by God in the Scriptures of the Old and New Testaments, and in the living experience of the Church of Christ.

The Conference would draw attention to the significant testimony so widely borne by missionary experience that where Jews have genuinely accepted Christ, they have very frequently stated that the main influence leading them to Christ has been the consistent life, or an act of loving service, of some true disciple of our Lord.

Recalling the promise that "they that wait upon the Lord shall receive their strength; they shall mount up with wings as eagles; they shall run and not be weary, and they shall walk and not faint," the Conference commends its members and all fellow-workers in the cause of winning the Jews for Christ unto Him that is able to keep them from falling and to present them faultless before the presence of His glory with exceeding joy.

VIII. Co-operation

The World Conference wishes to place on record its recognition of the gratifying progress already made in co-operation among various agencies engaged in Christian work among the Jews, and recognises that this Conference itself constitutes possibly the best illustration of this fact and affords fresh and convincing evidence both of the need and of the desire for wider and more fruitful co-operative effort. The Conference further recognises that it will fall short of its highest possibilities unless steps be taken to make all that it has stood for permanent in the life and activities of the Churches.

The Conference considers it most fortunate that there is in the International Missionary Council an organisation which has not only made this Conference possible, but which also provides an agency whereby it can communicate to the various societies as well as to the national missionary organisations the findings of the Conference for their consideration and for such action as they may deem it desirable to take.

I. We appeal, therefore, to the International Missionary Council to consider at its first meeting how it can draw more closely together in co-operative action the various Societies, and how it can make the work among Jews more central in the plans and sacrificial devotion of the Churches.

II. We would request the Council to make the findings and recommendations of the Conference known to the Churches and agencies concerned, and likewise to devise some permanent means for ensuring continued joint consultation on the part of those at work among Jews, for their sharing of insight, knowledge and experience on common problems, for united exploration and research in matters in which joint action may prove to be desirable, and for such other co-operative activities as may from time to time be desired.

III. In view of the opened doors for enlarged service which have been brought to the attention of the Conference, in view of the magnitude and difficulty of the task to be performed, and in view of limited forces in men and money, the Conference would urge the desirability of conserving and liberating all possible resources through avoiding unnecessary duplication of effort and lack of concert in planning.

IV. The Conference requests the International Missionary Council to invite the co-operation in their respective spheres of the World Student Christian Federation, the World Committee of the Young Men's Christian Association, and the World Committee of the Young Women's

Christian Association, as well as of the youth movements within the Churches.

V. Pending consideration and action by the International Missionary Council, the Conference recommends the continuation of the Committee of Arrangements as it may be constituted by the Business Committee, in order to provide for any necessary and interim action.

IX. Work among Jewish Women

I. Among the social evolutions taking place in the world to-day none is more pervasive and potential than that which affects the status and activities of women. The women of Jewry are particularly influenced, not only by this world-wide movement, but also by the changing ideals and the breakdown of social standards within their own people. The wider social freedom and the liberation of her intellectual and spiritual nature makes of the Jewish woman a centre of the new power either for good or ill. There is, therefore, the more urgent need for bringing the women of this great people into contact with the spiritual dynamic and the ethical teaching of Jesus Christ.

II. We recommend that this need be laid on the hearts of Christian women, and that literature be selected or prepared for the use of women's missionary agencies which will acquaint them with conditions now obtaining in the Jewish world.

III. Provision should be made for more women workers, who, by life and word, may interpret Christ to His people. Biblewomen, visiting nurses, welfare workers, teachers, women doctors, industrial instructors, directors of social centres and hostels are needed.

IV. Baby clinics, dispensaries, nurseries, sewing classes, night classes, reading rooms, clubs, study groups, mothers' rest-camps, and employment bureaus afford opportunities for contact and service.

V. For younger women we suggest the necessity for

hostels in factory, shop and educational centres. For all such service women of fine calibre and training are required.

VI. We urge that work among women in any Jewish Mission field can never be carried on with entire success until there is adequate representation of women on boards directing such work, and especially on such committees as deal with the selection of candidates.

VII. We recommend that trained Jewish-Christian women be used wherever possible in the evangelisation of their people, and that missionary groups be organised among Jewish-Christian women to challenge their commitment to the world-wide missionary enterprise.

THE FINDINGS OF THE WARSAW CONFERENCE

I. Evangelisation and Message

As a Conference on the Christian Message to the Jews, we desire to put on record our goodwill and friendly feeling toward the Jewish people; we deplore the long record of injustice and ill-usage of Jews on the part of professedly Christian people; we declare such conduct to be a violation of the teaching and spirit of Christ, and we call upon Churches and Christians everywhere to oppose injustice and ill-usage of Jews and to express to them by word and act the spirit of Jesus Christ our Lord, their Saviour and ours.

I. We are convinced that the Church of Christ is facing a new day in Jewish Missions. The signs of the times awaken new hope for the future.

(*a*) Economic and social progress is evident among the Jews in nearly all countries. The passing of the Ghetto is a fact.

(*b*) In most countries there is a passion for education, not of the old Synagogue-type, but such as is afforded in State schools.

(*c*) There is a new attitude of mind toward the great fact of history—Jesus Christ.

(*d*) The rise of a new national consciousness, as exemplified by Zionism and other movements, implies a protest against unworthy assimilation, and maintains the hope of a great destiny for this people.

(*e*) But some of the new developments in Judaism may be fraught with great danger to the world, unless they are directed into Christian channels.

For these reasons we are convinced that there is a special

urgency to-day to evangelise the whole Jewish people—the fifteen and a half million Jews of the present-day "dispersion." This very dispersion is a call of God to His Church.

The basis and authority of Missions to the Jews rest primarily on the special command and love of our Lord Jesus. It is an undoubted fact that neglect of Jewish Missions would deprive the Church of the great spiritual gifts latent in the Jewish people and result in spiritual dearth for the Church Universal.

II. We bring to the Jews the Gospel of the love of God shown to us in Jesus of Nazareth, seen of men, crucified, risen and glorified. He is the fulfilment of the Law—the Redeemer of mankind from sin and death; He is the fulfilment of the hopes spoken by the Prophets—the true Messiah; He is the Incarnate Word of God.

Jesus Christ is the "spiritual centre" from which alone the Jews will derive true inspiration and national redemption. He alone is "the true consolation of Israel" for which they have longed in their sorrows; He alone is the bond which will once again bind up their broken national body. The Kingdom of Heaven which He came to bring is the "ideal Society"; only by carrying out His teaching and in His spirit can humanity attain its goal.

We are called upon to bring this good news in absolute faith and in a spirit of true sympathy, striving to comprehend the spiritual longing of the Jews.

III. In view of the wide distribution of Jews in many Christian lands and their residence within the bounds of Church parishes, we recognise the providential opportunity thus afforded to preach the Gospel to our Jewish neighbours. Therefore we urge upon the pastors of such churches the importance of Jewish Evangelism by the testimony and the example of the church-members and the appointment, training and support, by the local church or Church Synods, of workers for service among the Jewish community.

IV. In presenting our message we may not overlook the

seven and a half million Jewish women and girls and their special claims.

Though among the Orthodox, the Jewish woman has been for centuries relegated to a subordinate place in religious matters and is greatly ignorant of the spiritual, as distinguished from the ceremonial side of religion, yet as wife and mother her influence is intense. She can be a source of ignorant and fanatical opposition to the Christian message ; she can also be a channel in the home for the free flow of Christian influence under which she may have come in earlier life. The great ideal to hold up before Jewish womanhood is the acceptance of Jesus Christ and that they follow Him like those Jewish women of old who ministered to Him and were the first to proclaim His resurrection.

V. We call attention to the special need and opportunity for evangelism among educated and cultured Jews, both men and women in the great University centres. Separated from their homes and the Synagogue, these student classes are often in great loneliness. They are the leaders of the future, their minds are remarkably open to new ideas, and they therefore can be readily influenced by suitable constructive Christian apologetic in the form of literature, but even more by sympathy and Christian help of every kind.

VI. Finally, we call attention to the finding of the Budapest Conference on Baptism, and in general we endorse it, as a wise statement regarding this very difficult problem :—

" We call attention to the fact that baptism, prematurely performed, often makes the baptised Jew a stumbling-block to other Jews, and a reproach to the Mission and the Church.

" When a Jew applies for baptism, the missionary should do his utmost to test his profession and observe his life, lest there be any ulterior motives in his mind.

" The aim of missions is not to 'make propaganda,' but to win souls for Christ and lead them to holy living.

The missionary ought, therefore, to show special caution in admitting for baptism those for whom there is no community of Christian people prepared to receive the converts and give them the necessary spiritual help and guidance. A period of wise and careful instruction should precede baptism, and, where possible, an accurate register of baptisms should be kept."

II. Missionary Methods

I. The methods of reaching the Jews with the Gospel are many and varied. It is impossible to lay down any definite scheme to be adopted in a centre as the best method of approach, as every station has to be considered according to its own local needs and possibilities. We would, however, recommend that the best results can be obtained—

(*a*) By consecrated personal work on the part of all Christian workers showing to the Jews the Spirit of Christ by kindliness, truth and love.

(*b*) By the preaching and teaching of the Gospel of Jesus Christ in churches and buildings specially set apart for the work of evangelisation; also by propagating the Gospel by means of itineracy, and lectures in available halls away from the neighbourhood of mission centres.

(*c*) By preparation and distribution of special literature. It is essential that literature should be specially prepared for the different types of Jews in their own or in the language of the countries where they reside, and for Christians about Jews. We recommend that specially chosen literature prepared for Christians should be used among the more highly educated Jews.

II. We recommend, further, that this Conference should support the proposal of the Budapest Conference that the International Missionary Council be requested to secure the appointment of four co-operating Committees, representing work in Eastern Europe, Central Europe, Great Britain and North America, with a co-ordinating Secretary appointed by the International Missionary Council, in order that such literature may be prepared and issued.

III. Other methods of approach with the view of reaching the Home and whole life of the Jew which have proved possible and successful in many centres are :—

(*a*) Educational work.
(*b*) Medical work.
(*c*) Industrial work.
(*d*) Homes for Enquirers and Converts.
(*e*) Bible Study Circles for Students.
(*f*) Community Centres.
(*g*) Summer Camps.
(*h*) Kino, Radio, etc.
(*i*) Home visiting.
(*j*) Open-air work.

As far as these methods are based on philanthropy, care must be taken that they do not tend to demoralise, and everything which appears to denationalise the Jew should be avoided. Whatever method is adopted and found to meet the needs of the particular centre should be made as efficient as the funds of the agency carrying on the work will permit.

IV. We recommend that there should be co-operation in definite branches of activity so as to secure the best possible results.

III. The Training of Workers

Jewish Missions are to-day face to face with great problems, and the lack of suitable workers is tremendous. To win and to train witnesses for Christ to Israel are, accordingly, matters of vital importance, and regarding them the following considerations are put forward :—

I. On the question of the respective functions of Jewish and Gentile Christians in Jewish Evangelisation—

(*a*) No one is fitted by nature for work in the Kingdom of God. Mission agents must be prayed for by the Church, called of God, equipped and fittingly prepared for the work. The varieties of the several national and religious groups, which are conditioned by birth, education, environment, by sex, and by special personal gifts, are to be recognised. There is, however, no essential difference between workers of Gentile and Jewish origin. All are one in Christ. The chief thing is that the missionary be a Christian personality, who in love wills to be all things to all men.

(*b*) Accordingly, Jewish and Gentile Christians are fitted for work of every kind; both are wanted and may claim equal rights; they should supplement one another and serve God with the gifts with which He has endowed them.

II. A thorough biblical, theological and general training is assumed, but in order to meet the changed conditions within Jewry, particular attention should be given to—

(*a*) The acquisition of the Hebrew and Yiddish languages, where the situation requires them;

(*b*) Knowledge of the teaching of the Talmud, of the history of the Jews to the present day, of the religious and national movements among the Jews (Chassidism, Reform Judaism, and Zionism), and of the latest Jewish literature.

III. Regarding the type of training and facilities for the same—

1. (*a*) For all regular workers (directors, missionaries, colporteurs, nurses, Biblewomen, etc.), careful training, appropriate for their several spheres of activity, is required, and, as a rule, it should not, in the case of leaders, be inferior to that of the ministers and clergy of the Churches,

(*b*) For Europe two training centres are regarded as necessary: for the West, the approved Institutum Judaicum Delitzschianum at Leipzig; and, for the East, the newly founded Institution in Warsaw, should be encouraged and developed. Both are at the service of all Churches and Societies. Similar Institutions should be opened in other parts where needed.

(*c*) In order to maintain the efficiency of workers and

to give them fresh stimulus, continuation courses should be held from time to time.

2. (*a*) To train friends and voluntary workers and to awaken interest for Jewish Missions in congregations, special missionary courses and vacation schools for pastors, teachers, evangelists and interested Church members should be arranged.

(*b*) To awaken and win the interest and help of students in the cause of Jewish Evangelisation, an appeal should be addressed to the Christian organisations at work among them.

(*c*) Lastly, a new Handbook on Jewish Missions, similar to the Manuals published by the Board of Missionary Preparation in New York, and Dr Gustav Dalman's Text-book on Jewish Missions, should be made available for the help of all who are concerned with Jewish Missions.

IV. That these important objects may be attained, closer co-operation of existing organisations is necessary.

IV. Occupation of the Field

The Jewish problem is a complex one, Jews being found in almost every nation and in every station in life. Yet they have an underlying unity which demands unity of treatment. Their importance, moreover, throughout the world is out of all proportion to their numbers, either on account of the position which they occupy in the intellectual, commercial and political life of the lands where they dwell, or on account of the relation in which they stand to non-Christian movements and forces, such as Mohammedanism, etc.

In surveying the field of Jewish Evangelisation, with its vast unoccupied areas, broken with particular spheres relatively overmanned, this Conference is impressed with the urgent need for re-planning, taking the whole field into view and paying due attention to areas of special importance. It therefore makes the following recommendations :—

I. Special and immediate attention should be paid to unoccupied territories such as those of Central, Eastern and South-Eastern Europe, and of South America.

II. As the unoccupied territory is so large that it cannot be occupied effectively in the immediate future, this Conference recommends that from select central points efforts should be made to evangelise surrounding districts, not merely by means of colporteurs, but also by means of well-equipped itinerant evangelists.

III. Special attention is directed to the thousands of Jewish students in Colleges and Universities throughout the world who have scarcely been touched as yet by the Christian evangel.

IV. This Conference calls upon the Christian Churches of the Continent of Europe where there is a Jewish population, to consider their special responsibility for the work of evangelising the Jews who are in their midst. This Conference would also urge those Churches that have not yet taken any part in the work of evangelising the Jewish people, to take hold of the present-day opportunity and claim a share in the privilege and responsibility of this important work.

V. This Conference requests the International Missionary Council to make a thorough survey of the Jewish field, so that information may be provided for the guidance of Societies and Churches in laying down future policy.

V. Spiritual Power

I. The Conference is deeply conscious that spiritual power in its fullness is essential in the work of Jewish Evangelisation. Lack of power in the past is due among other reasons to the following :—

(*a*) There has been a lack of interest, fervour and prayer in the heart of the Church with regard to specific Jewish Evangelisation. We thank God for all devoted service in this cause in the past, but realise that, as compared with the grave problems of the situation, our past work has not always been well conceived, wisely planned, and whole-heartedly undertaken. This has involved an undoubted loss of power.

(*b*) The sins of Christendom against the Jew which we frankly confess—past persecution, and present indifference and ignorance—have hindered the work, foreclosed opportunities, shut doors that were ajar, and dissipated power. Hence the Church has often failed to fulfil the mind of Jesus Christ and make use of God's resources.

(*c*) The defective example of the average Christian life and conduct has hindered the manifestation of the power of Jesus Christ to redeem and bless. As the best argument for Jesus is a worthy Christian life, so the worst enemy of spiritual power is an inconsistent life.

II. This Conference realises with gratitude that, notwithstanding the difficulties of the work of Jewish Evangelisation, the sufficiency of the worker is not of himself, but of God. The risen Christ is invested with all power in heaven and on earth. Through the might of His quickening spirit He is able to subdue all things unto Himself; and He has promised to be with His servants, in sustaining and vitalising energy, even unto the end of the world.

III. There are divinely appointed means and channels of spiritual power, both for ourselves, and for the world through us.

1. For ourselves in the cultivation of our own life, it cannot be emphasised too strongly that all spiritual power comes only from a constant connection with the source of power. The means towards this are obvious—a regular study of Holy Scripture, the practice of prayer and meditation, a realisation of the purpose of God for His ancient people, the inspiration derived from the example of our Lord and the prophets and apostles, a confident claiming of God's promises of fulfilment, and a reliant personal faith. We feel that this faith, while facing the weighty problems with clear eyes and refusing to minimise the difficulties, must also realise the powers that are on our

side, and must believe that we can do all things through Jesus Christ.

2. We must seek to make Spiritual Power operative on others, through us as God's servants. It is difficult to define or even enumerate methods of spiritual influence, but the Conference suggests the following as being essential to success :—

(*a*) A consecrated life, as the best commendation of the Gospel.

(*b*) Human gifts and qualities of mind and heart trained and devoted to Christ's service.

(*c*) A clear view of the ultimate object in our Christian service, to win the Jews for Jesus Christ.

(*d*) In view of the spiritual perils due to loneliness, it is recommended that the Lord's method be followed by sending workers out in twos.

IV. Spiritual Power is dissipated by division and disunion. We believe that the manifestation of a united front would bring an accession of power. We believe that fuller co-operation, consultation, fellowship and prayer would result in better work and deeper enthusiasm, and would encourage all lonely workers with a sense of Christian fellowship.

We believe that under God the irresistible power manifested by the disciples and martyrs of apostolic days, whose witness turned the world upside down, may still be ours in our present need, and will always attend the triumphant proclamation of the apostolic witness to the crucified, risen and living Lord.

Finally, the members of the Conference, realising that in labouring for the evangelisation of Israel they are working in the line of God's revealed purpose, urge upon all who are so engaged to persevere in their task with hopefulness and courage, commending them to Him who is able to do exceeding abundantly above all that we ask or think, according to the power that worketh in us.

BESCHLÜSSE DER BUDAPESTER KONFERENZ

I. Evangelisation und Botschaft

I. Die Konferenz erkennt die Verantwortlichkeit jeder Kirche und jedes einzelnen Christen den Juden gegenüber, die in ihrer Mitte wohnen, an. Es besteht aber auch ein dringendes und wachsendes Bedürfnis nach einer eigenen Evangelisation unter den Juden der Welt. Diese Arbeit muss sich direkt an die Juden richten, und die Arbeiter sollen eigens dazu ausgebildet werden. Die Notwendigkeit und Dringlichkeit dieser Arbeit sollen der ganzen christlichen Kirche feierlich ans Herz gelegt werden.

Folgende Gründe legen solche Evangelisation nahe—

(*a*) Die Autorität der Schrift und die Liebe Jesu zu seinem Volke.

(*b*) Das eigentümliche Leben und die Umwelt der Juden.

(*c*) Ihre geistige Denkart und Veranlagung.

(*d*) Die gegenwärtige, einzigartige Gelegenheit, die mit der Erschütterung ihres alten Glaubens gegeben ist.

(*e*) Die Anzeichen dafür, dass solche Mission vielerorten willkommen ist.

(*f*) Der geistige Gewinn, den der jüdische Glaubenseifer der christlichen Kirche einbringen wird.

Wir legen den Christen überall ans Herz, Busse zu tun für die Vorurteile gegenüber dem jüdische Volk und für die Judenverfolgungen. Diese Dinge gehören leider noch nicht der Vergangenheit an, und in einigen Ländern werden sogar sich zum Christentum bekennende Organisationen damit identifiziert. Wir glauben, dass alle unchristliche Behandlung der Juden und alle Rassenvorurteile für die

Juden ein grosses Hindernis sind, die christliche Botschaft anzunehmen.

II. Unsere Botschaft an die Juden besteht in der Verkündigung Jesu Christi, der uns durch die Liebe Gottes gegeben, gekreuzigt, auferstanden und verherrlicht ist. Er ist die Erfüllung des Gesetzes, und der wahre Messias, das fleischgewordene Wort, der Erlöser der Welt, der Erretter von der Sünde, der Israel zu seiner Bestimmung bringt, nämlich, ein Segen für die ganze Menschheit zu werden.

Diese Botschaft muss mit Demut und Liebe und in opferwilligem Dienen verkündet werden, so dass die Juden von einer blossen Messiaserwartung oder vom Beharren in Selbstgerechtigkeit zu wahrer Busse und zum Bekenntnis der Sünde erweckt werden. Sie müssen für die Erneuerung des Herzens beten, damit sie durch Jesu Christi Opfertod Vergebung erhalten und seine treuen Nachfolger werden.

III. In der Religion Israels sind Kulturwerte und moralische Grundsätze vorhanden, die in anderen, nicht-christlichen Religionen nicht vorhanden sind. Die Juden und die Christen haben das Alte Testament als Urkunde der Offenbarung Gottes an die Menschheit gemeinsam, ein Erbe, das andere, nicht-christliche Religionen nicht haben. Der Jude hat auch als Eigenbesitz ein Bewusstsein von seiner besonderen Stellung in Gottes Plan zur Erlösung der Welt.

Daher, beim Herantreten an die jüdische Religion muss man, zum Unterschied von anderen nicht-christlichen Religionen, dieses religiöse Erbgut Israels in Rechnung setzen. Der Unterschied zwischen Anhängern anderer nicht-christlichen Religionen und Anhängern des Judentums für die religiöse Botschaft besteht darin, dass der eine durch Jesus Christus zu Gott geführt wird, während der andere zu Jesus Christus aus seinem vorhandenen, aber ungeläuterten Gottesglauben gelangt.

IV. Im Blick auf die grosse Ausdehnung des Arbeitsgebietes und die verschiedenen Typen der Juden, unter denen wir zu arbeiten haben, glauben wir, dass die anzuwendenden Methoden der jeweiligen Umwelt und Kultur angepasst sein müssen. Es gibt keine einheitliche Methode für alle Verhältnisse. Das gilt auch für die Darbietung unserer Botschaft. Jede Methode, die unnötig den jüdischen Widerstand weckt, sollte vermieden werden.

V. Wir machen auf die Tatsache aufmerksam, dass durch eine zu früh gewährte Taufe der getaufte Jude oft zu einem Aergernis für andere Juden wird und zu einem Vorwurf für die Mission und für die Kirche.

Wenn ein Jude die Taufe verlangt, soll der Missionar sorgfältig den Ernst seines Wollens, sowie sein Leben prüfen, um gewiss zu sein, dass ihn keine abwegigen Beweggründe leiten.

Das Ziel der Mission besteht nicht darin, Propaganda zu machen, sondern Seelen für Christus zu gewinnen und sie zu einem Leben in der Heiligung zu führen. Der Missionar soll daher besondere Vorsicht bei der Taufe dort anwenden, wo keine christliche Gemeinde den Bekehrten aufnimmt und ihm die notwendige geistliche Hilfe und Führung gibt. Der Taufe soll ein wohldurchdachter und sorgfältiger Unterricht vorangehen. Wo es möglich ist, wird ein genaues Taufregister geführt.

II. Christliche Erziehung

I. Als Diener Christi, der die Kleinen in Israel in seine Arme nahm und segnete, haben die Glieder der christlichen Kirchen die Pflicht, darauf bedacht zu sein, die Herzen der Jugend des heutigen Israel für diesen Heiland zu gewinnen, an Dem sie alles Recht hat. Zu diesem Ende sollten, wo immer die Möglichkeit dafür besteht, Schulen und Internate weiter erhalten oder eingerichtet werden. Dazu bedarf es dringend eines Ueberblickes über das ganze, schon bearbeitete und noch unbearbeitete Gebiet.

Was solche Schulen anzustreben haben, ist (*a*) die Schaffung einer christlichen Atmosphäre in der Schule und die Hinleitung der jugendlichen Gemüter zur Person Christi, und (*b*) die bestmögliche Ausbildung in den weltlichen Fächern. Solche Schulen werden sowohl für die Kinder der Konvertiten, als für die Juden, die eine christliche oder höhere sittliche Ausbildung ihrer Kinder begehren, die nötige Erziehung zu besorgen haben. Sie werden an Orten, wo eine entsprechende Erziehung nicht gewährleistet ist, oder wo der Antisemitismus den Juden die öffentlichen Schulen nahezu unerträglich macht, einen Tatbeweis christlicher Liebe darstellen. Sie werden ferner die Jugend Israels vor religiöser Gleichgiltigkeit oder gar Feindschaft gegen die Religion bewahren helfen, die sie der grössten Lebensgüter beraubt und zu einer Gefahr für die Gesellschaft macht.

II. Der Aufwand an Zeit und Geld für solche Schulen rechtfertigt sich durch seine Erfolge. Unmittelbare Erfolge sind : (*a*) dass Zöglinge sich taufen lassen, sei es mit Zustimmung ihrer Eltern, oder nach Erreichung des landesgesetzlich vorgeschriebenen Alters ; (*b*) die grosse Anzahl heimlicher Christusnachfolger, die aus derlei Schulen hervorgegangen sind. Als mittelbare Erfolge sind anzusehen : (*a*) die freundlichere Stellung gegen das Christentum und die grössere Achtung vor der Mission, wie sie durch Berührung mit christlicher Lehre und echtem christlichen Leben und Lieben angeregt werden ; (*b*) die Gelegenheit zu missionarischem Dienst, die sich dadurch ergibt.

III. Es müssen folgende wesentliche Forderungen aufgestellt werden :—

(*a*) Die Schulen müssen mit den Schulen gleicher Art in dem betreffenden Lande jeden Vergleich aushalten. Daher müssen die Lehrkräfte die volle Befähigung zum Unterricht besitzen. Gebäude und Einrichtung müssen ganz zeitgemäss sein und der Lehrplan ganz auf der Höhe stehen.

(*b*) Soweit es nur irgend angeht, muss sich der Lehrkörper aus Leuten zusammensetzen, die durch Lehre und Leben die Kinder zu Christus zu führen gewillt sind.

(*c*) Es muss die Freiheit gewährleistet sein, das Neue Testament und die christlichen Glaubenswahrheiten ganz und unvermindert zu lehren, und es müssen Lehrer da sein, die es zu ihrer besonderen Aufgabe gemacht haben, jüdischen Kindern die christliche Wahrheit zu vermitteln.

(*d*) Der Lehrgang muss so eingerichtet sein, dass die Zöglinge so lange als möglich unter christlichem Einfluss bleiben.

(*e*) Es ist alles zu vermeiden, was die Zöglinge ihrem Volke entfremden könnte. Als Lehrgegenstand käme unter Umständen auch die jüdische Geschichte und das Hebräische in Betracht, letzteres besonders in dem Falle, dass die Eltern es wünschen.

(*f*) Man hat dafür zu sorgen und die nötigen Lehrkräfte dafür auszuwählen, dass die Verbindung mit den Kindern nach ihrem Abgang von der Schule aufrecht erhalten bleibe, sei es durch Klubs oder Kränzchen oder durch ständigen Briefwechsel. Wenn nötig, sind die, die ihren Glauben an Christus bekannt haben, in eigenen Heimstätten unterzubringen.

(*g*) Mit Hinblick auf die Zukunft der Knaben und der Mädchen, sollte die Mission in der Regel Schulen für beide Geschlechter einrichten.

(*h*) Die Arbeit in der Schule sollte von den Lehrern und von besonders bestellten Aufsichtübenden in den Familien der Kinder fortgesetzt und ergänzt werden.

IV. Mit folgenden Problemen hätte man sich eingehend zu befassen :—

(*a*) Die Stellung der Behörden zu den Missionsschulen.

(*b*) Die öffentliche Meinung in einigen Ländern betreffs früher Heiraten und des vorzeitigen Abgangs von der Schule.

(*c*) Die hohen Kosten der Erhaltung von Missionsschulen, in solchen Ländern, wo das Bildungswesen auf sehr hoher Stufe steht, oder wo die Lebenshaltung auf sehr tiefer Stufe steht.

V. Das alles erschöpft die Pflicht der christlichen Kirche an der Jugend Israels noch nicht. Kirchen und Missionen sollten sich vielmehr alle Mühe geben, die jüdische Jugend ihrer Umgebung zu gewinnen und zu beeinflussen. Dafür gibt es Mittel, wie Spielplätze, Lehrstunden und Turnstunden, Sommererholungsstätten, Ferien-Bibelschulen, usw., alles das in Verbindung mit ganz bestimmter christlicher Belehrung, aber bei ganz freiwilliger Beteiligung.

VI. Es ist aufs höchste zu wünschen, dass alle unter der Jugend beider Geschlechter wirkenden christlichen Organisationen, wie die christliche Studentenvereinigung, die christlichen Vereine junger Männer und junger Mädchen, Pfadfinder beiden Geschlechtes, usw., ermutigt werden, die jüdische Jugend in den Bereich ihrer Tätigkeit aufzunehmen.

III. Aerztliche Mission; Philantropische Tätigkeit; und "Gemeinschafts-mittelpunkte" (Community Centres)

I. In Bezug auf die missionsärztliche Arbeit:—

1. Die Grundsätze des christlichen Glaubens fordern die Erfüllung der Pflicht, für den Körper wie für die Seele Sorge zu tragen, entsprechend dem Verhalten Jesu Christi.

2. Diese Grundsätze verpflichten die christliche Mission für beiderlei Nöte zu sorgen, soweit es die örtlichen Verhältnisse und die Mittel erlauben.

3. Missionskrankenhäuser sollen überall mustergiltig eingerichtet werden; diese Anstalten müssen zugleich den besonderen Charakter von Stätten der Mission tragen, und, wenigstens in den grössern Anstalten, soll der ärztliche Dienst durch andere für evangelistische Arbeit specifisch angestellte Arbeitskräfte ergänzt werden.

4. Alle Patienten sollen eingeladen und ermuntert werden, die Gottesdienste zu besuchen, in denen die evangelische Verkündigung dargeboten wird. Unter gewissen Umständen mag es wünschenswert sein, den Besuch dieser Gottesdienste zur Bedingung für die Aufnahme zu machen, aber auf dieser Bedingung soll nicht unter allen Umständen bestanden werden.

5. Bemittelte Patienten sollen für die ärztlichen Hilfeleistungen, für Kost und andere Spesen nach Kräften, entweder ganz oder teilweise, bezahlen. Unbemittelten Patienten sollen die Dienste und Mittel der Anstalt unentgeltlich zur Verfügung stehen.

6. Polikliniken, staatlich anerkannte Hebammen- und Gemeindeschwestern gelten als normale Ergänzung eines normalen Missionskrankenhauses. Diese Einrichtungen erweisen sich als überaus nützlich, auch dort, wo keine Krankenhäuser vorhanden sind. Was über Bezahlung in Punkt 5. gesagt ist, gilt auch für Punkt 6.

7. Die Resultate der christlich-ärztlichen Mission sind durchweg günstig und ermunternd.

II. Ueber Heime :—1. Heime für Juden, die Jesum kennen lernen wollen (Enquirers), sind von grosser Nützlichkeit. Diese sollen jedoch von Missionsbehörden oder Gesellschaften gegründet und erhalten werden.

2. Heime für Judenchristen :—Auch diese sind von grossem Segen ; jedoch, in Anbetracht der Unterhaltungskosten und der Arbeitsschwierigkeiten, ist die Eröffnung solcher Anstalten in grösserer Zahl unausführbar, es sei denn auf der Basis eines internationalen oder interevangelischen Zusammenwirkens. Die Internationale Hebrew-Christian Allianz scheint, wegen der Herkunft und der Erfahrung ihrer Mitglieder, für die Gründung und Führung solcher Heime besonders berufen zu sein.

III. " Gemeinschafts - Mittelpunkte " (Community Centres) :—An gewissen Orten Nordamerikas unter einer gemischten Bevölkerung von verschiedenen Religionen und Nationen haben christliche " Gemeinschafts-Mittelpunkte " sich als überaus segensreich erwiesen.

IV. Andere philantropische Mittel :—Andere Werke der Barmherzigkeit, wie Heime für alte Judenchristen oder für Waisenkinder, ruhen auf den Grundsätzen der allgemeinen christlichen Wohltätigkeit, sind aber in der Judenmission auch wünschenswert, vorausgesetzt dass die Mission für solche besonderen Zwecke über reiche Mittel verfügt. Empfänger von Unterstützungen die körperlich fähig sind, sollen als Gegenleistung etwas Arbeit verrichten.

IV. Christliche Literatur

I. Es gibt eine grosse Literatur, die, ohne besondere Rücksicht auf die nationale oder religiöse Umwelt der Juden zu nehmen, geeignet ist, bei den Juden Verständnis für das Christentum zu wecken. Man sollte eine Auswahl der besten Bücher treffen, die eine Annäherung an das gebildete Judentum zu fördern geeignet sind.

II. Von der Literatur, die unmittelbar zur Beeinflussung der Juden geschrieben ist, ist ein Teil veraltet, ein anderer unbrauchbar geworden wegen seines polemischen, übertrieben irenischen, oder anfechtbar apologetischen Charakters. Dergleichen Tendenzen sind nicht zu entbehren. Sie müssen aber aus einem Geist verständnisvoller Sympathie kommen. Wieder ein anderer hat bleibende Bedeutung, weil er ewige Wahrheiten verbreitet. Der von Dr Strack begonnene, von Canon Lukyn Williams fortgesetzte Katalog soll weitergeführt werden. Die Herausgabe dieses Katalogs wird empfohlen.

III. Für neu zu schaffende Literatur werden folgende Vorschläge gemacht :—

(*a*) Es ist neue Literatur erwünscht für die verschiedenen Typen innerhalb der Judenheit : (1) orthodoxe, (2) reformerische, (3) sozialfortschrittliche Juden. In jeder Gruppe soll auch auf die Frauen Bedacht genommen werden.

(*b*) Einer besonderen Literatur bedürfen wir für die dem Materialismus verfallenen Juden, für Schulkinder und Studenten.

(*c*) Auf die verschiedene Kulturumgebung und die Landessprachen der jüdischen Gruppen ist Rücksicht zu nehmen.

IV. Auf folgenden literarischen Gebieten sind besonders neue Bücher und Schriften erwünscht :—

Anfänge des Christentums, einschliesslich " Leben Jesu ";

Epochen der Kirchengeschichte; Christliche Glaubens und Sittenlehre; Biographien, insbesondere auch von hervorragenden Judenchristen; Erbauungsbücher, einschliesslich Gebetbücher und mehrsprachige Liederbücher.

Solche Literatur brauchen wir in Buch- und Broschürenform, wenn nötig volkstümlich gefasst und illustriert.

V. Literatur über Juden für Christen:—Die Konferenz emfiehlt eine Zentrale zu schaffen, die eine Uebersicht geben möchte über Literatur, die den Christen Verständnis für die Geisteswelt der Juden verschaffen kann und ihre Verantwortlichkeit gegenüber der Judenheit zum Ausdruck bringt. Es wird die Notwendigkeit betont, eine neue zeitgemässe und billige Literatur über die Juden zu schaffen.

VI. Fühlung mit den Missionaren unter den Juden:—Die Konferenz empfiehlt, es möchten die Judenmissionare durch ihre Gesellschaften auf Literatur aufmerksam gemacht werden, die ihnen in den verschiedenen Gebieten nützlich sein kann. Zu diesem Zweck soll durch den Zentralsekretär ein Bureau für Austausch und Vermittlung solcher Literatur geschaffen werden.

VII. Zusammenarbeit:—Diese Bedürfnisse können nur dann mit Sparsamkeit und der nötigen Wirkungskraft befriedigt werden, wenn eine gute Zusammenarbeit hergestellt wird.

Die Zusammenarbeit soll sich auf folgende Punkte erstrecken—

(*a*) Uebersicht über die verschiedenen Gebiete und ihre Bedürfnisse vom Gesichtspunkt der Literaturbeschaffung.

(*b*) Beschaffung geeigneter Verfasser und Uebersetzer.

(*c*) Verbindung mit angesehenen Verlegerfirmen, die solche Literatur veröffentlichen.

(*d*) Methoden des Vertriebes durch den Handel, Missionsarbeiter, Kolporteure, und Bibelfrauen.

Wir empfehlen die Schaffung eines zentralen Bureaus für Zusammenarbeit, das unter dem Internationalen Missionsrat stehen würde. Es muss in Fühlung stehen (*a*) mit den hauptsächlichen intellektuellen und akademischen Zentren, deren Mitwirkung für Beschaffung solcher Literatur nützlich erscheinen mag; (*b*) mit den verschiedenen christlichen Organisationen, die unter den Juden arbeiten.

Wir ersuchen den Internationalen Missionsrat, vier Kommitees zu bestellen, deren Arbeit durch einen Zentralsekretär in Einklang gebracht werden soll. Diese vier Kommitees vertreten die Arbeit in Osteuropa, Zentraleuropa, Grossbritannien, und Nordamerika. Der Zentralsekretär soll durch den Internationalen Missionsrat gewählt und angestellt werden.

VIII. Finanzen:—Um die Ausgaben für die Besoldung des Zentralsecretärs sowie, soweit nötig, die Honorierung der Autoren, die Veröffentlichung und den Vertrieb der Literatur zu decken, bedarf es eines Fonds, auch wenn ein freiwilliger Secretär gefunden werden kann. Ein solcher Fond kann nicht gut durch einen öffentlichen Aufruf geschaffen werden, auch nicht durch Beträge der christlichen Organisationen, die unter Juden arbeiten. Eher könnte man ins Auge fassen, ob nicht von bedeutender privater Seite das Stammkapital aufgebracht werden kann, das nötig ist für den Anfang dieser Arbeit und die erste Probezeit, in der Hoffnung, dass später der Ertrag aus dem Verkauf der Literatur die Kosten der Organisation decken wird.

V. Die Besetzung des Missionsfeldes

I. Grosse Veränderungen gehen im Judentum, namentlich seit dem Weltkriege, vor sich, besonders eine neue Einstellung des Judentums selbst zu seinem religiösen Besitz und zur Person Jesu, die eine freundlichere, sympathisch interessierte genannt werden kann. Diese Veränderungen machen der christlichen Kirche das Studium der seelischen und intellektuellen Nöte und Bestrebungen des Judentums zur unabweisbaren Pflicht. Sie öffnen dem christlichen Dienst neue Türen und bieten eine günstige Gelegenheit, Christus in seiner ganzen Bedeutung seinem eigenen Volke vorzustellen.

Ein Volk von mehr denn 15 Millionen, weit zerstreut, scharfsinnig, reich begabt, und befähigt starke Kräfte für die Verkündigung des Evangeliums auszulösen, darf nicht vernachlässigt werden. Die gegenwärtige Lage ist ein klarer und dringender Ruf an die Kirche, in bisher vernachlässigte Gebiete einzudringen und sie wirksam zu besetzen, besonders dort, wo sich die grösste jüdische Bevölkerung befindet, wie in Ost-Europa und in den grösseren Städten von Nordamerika.

Es ist von grösster Wichtigkeit, bei der Besetzung der Missionsfelder nach einem wohlüberlegten Plane und mit wohldurchdachter Arbeitsmethode und Verwaltungstechnik vorzugehen. Zunächst sollten neue Kräfte benutzt werden, um die bestehenden Institutionen an strategisch wichtigen Mittelpunkten wirksam auszugestalten und ihnen einen weiteren Wirkungskreis zu geben.

II. Angesichts der Tatsache, dass dem jüdischen Missionsfelde bisher kein sorgfältiges und umfassendes Studium gewidmet wurde, drückt die Weltkonferenz den Wunsch aus, der Internationale Missionsrat möge—

(*a*) für das jüdische Gebiet dieselbe sorgfältige Ueberschau geben, wie das inbezug auf die mohammedanische Welt geschehen ist,

(*b*) mit solchen christlichen Institutionen Fühlung nehmen, die in grossem Stile Missionsarbeit an den Juden treiben können, damit bestimmte Gebiete, soweit das möglich ist, von vornherein an Gesellschaften verwiesen werden, die imstande sind, solche Gebiete zu besetzen; dadurch würde das “ Uebereinandergreifen ” und unerfreuliche Konkurrenz ausgeschaltet und das ganze Missionsfeld genügend besetzt werden.

III. Das Ghetto ist verschwunden. Die Juden beteiligen sich voll am Leben der modernen Welt. Millionen Juden leben jetzt inmitten der christlichen Gemeinden und im Schatten der christlichen Kirche. Diese Juden rekrutieren sich aus den verschiedensten Elementen und stehen grösstenteils ausserhalb des Arbeitsfeldes der vorhandenen Missionen. Sie bleiben ohne Evangelium, wenn die lokalen Kirchen diese Arbeit nicht selbst übernehmen. Diese Sachlage ist ein klarer Ruf Gottes an alle Kirchen, die solche Juden in ihrer Mitte haben, und auch an die Innere Mission, die Juden in ihren Dienst am Evangelium einzubeziehen.

IV. Angesichts der Tatsache, dass sich jüdische Studenten an solchen Universitäten, die keine Einschränkungen bei der Aufnahme machen, in unverhältnismässig grosser Zahl befinden; ferner angesichts des grossen Einflusses, den diese Studenten im späteren Leben auf allen öffentlichen Arbeitsgebieten besitzen, betont die Weltkonferenz mit allem Nachdruck, dass die Führer aller christlichen Studentenbewegungen auch die jüdischen Studenten in ihre Arbeit einschliessen sollen, und fordert die christ lichen Studenten auf, mit den jüdischen Studenten dieselben freundschaftlichen Beziehungen zu pflegen, wie es im Verkehr mit den anderen nichtchristlichen Studenten geschieht.

V. In der Annahme, dass die Zeit für uns Christen gekommen ist, unserer Stellung den Juden gegenüber Ausdruck zu verleihen, bedauert die Weltkonferenz die lange Geschichte der Ungerechtigkeit den Juden gegenüber und die Unbill, die den Juden von Namen-Christen angetan wurde. Die Konferenz erklärt, dass solche Ungerechtigkeit und Unbill eine Verletzung des Gebotes und des Geistes Christi ist, und sie ruft alle Kirchen und Christen auf, alle derartige Ungerechtigkeit und Unbill zu bekämpfen und den Juden durch Wort und Tat den Geist unseres Herrn Jesu Christus, unseres Erlösers, der auch der Juden Heiland ist, zu bezeugen.

Wir möchten unsere jüdischen Freunde nicht von ihrer Vergangenheit trennen und sie nicht ihres Erbes, das ja auch unser Erbe ist, berauben. Wir sind aber überzeugt, dass der Glaube an Jesus Christus, ihren Herrn und Erlöser, den Juden das wahre Heil und Glück verbirgt. Wir drücken fernerhin den Wunsch und die Hoffnung aus, dass durch die gemeinsame Anerkennung (allegiance) Jesu als Heiland und Erlöser eine Annäherung zwischen

Juden und Christen erreicht werde, die uns ermöglicht, gemeinsam vorwärts zu schreiten der Aufrichtung des Reiches Gottes auf Erden entgegen.

Addendum Ueber Palestina

Palestina enhält 1 Prozent von den Juden der Welt, jedoch wenn wir blosse Zahlen in Rechnung setzen, so gibt es im Heiligen Lande 12 Prozent der missionarischen Arbeitskräfte. Es ist eine Tatsache, dass es sehr viele Missionen, aber wenige Missionare im Sinne qualifizierter Kräfte gibt für direkte und fruchtbare Berührung mit den Juden Palestinas.

Die Probleme der übermässigen Besetzung beziehen sich eher auf Jerusalem, als auf Palestina als Ganzes. Die Tatsache, dass Jerusalem die heilige Stadt ist, bewirkt, dass sie unsere besondere Bemühung verdient, aber gleichermassen ist es bedeutsam, alle Schwärmerei mit der heiligen Stadt als unweise und unwürdig abzulehnen.

Die wirkliche strategische Bedeutung von Palestina bezieht sich nicht auf den Umfang, oder den voraussichtlichen Wachstum seiner jüdischen Bevölkerung, sondern auf neue lebendige Kulturkräfte des Judaismus, welche jetzt in Palestina eindringen, in den Personen stark hervortretender Literaten, Künstler, Lehrer, Denker und Journalisten. Diese haben sich nicht feindlich dem Christentum gezeigt, vielmehr umgekehrt. Unter diesen Gruppen hat sich bereits die Tendenz bemerkbar gemacht, die jüdische Haltung gegen Jesus Christus zu revidieren.

Es steht jetzt deutlich in unserer Macht, in Palestina die Atmosphäre in den Gebieten der Berührung zwischen Christen und Juden zu mildern und eine erhöhte Achtung für das Christentum herbeizuführen. Aber, wenn man ebenso fortfährt, wie man es bisher getan hat, mit den besten und einflussreichsten Elementen im modernen Judentum, das durch—gering zu sagen—unangemessene und manchmal unwürdige Repräsentation des Christentums zurückgestossen wurde, so muss eine zunehmende Verachtung für das Christentum gerade unter denen einziehen, deren Anschauung wir mit heisser Mühe zu beeinflussen suchen sollen.

Die Aufmerksamkeit sollte auf die künstlichen Verhältnisse in Palestina gelenkt werden. Das Land ist sozusagen ein Museum kirchlicher, kultureller und politischer Typen vom VII. bis zum XXI. Jahrhundert. Keiner von diesen führt sein natürliches Leben in seiner natürlichen Umgegung, sondern ein jeder ist in erster Reihe bemüht, sich selbst an dieser Quelle des jüdischen und des christlichen Glaubens im besten und charakteristischen Lichte zu zeigen. Auf diese Weise haben wir gute oder böse, mutmasslich repräsentative jüdische Typen vom alten oder vom modernen Judentum und von der jüdischen Zivilisation, und ebenso Typen von jeder Art des Christentums, alten und neuen, fortschrittlichen und unfortschrittlichen Schlages.

Wir sollten danach trachten, die Bedeutung und die Achtung des Christentums in Palestina nicht durch die Zahl solcher Arbeiter zu vermehren, deren ganze Qualifikation darin besteht, dass sie für den gefühlsmässigen Aufruf aus dem heiligen Lande empfänglich sind, sondern durch die Anstrengungen der Kirche und der Gesellschaften alles, was in ihrer Kraft liegt, zu tun, um die Wirksamkeit der bestehenden Institutionen zu erhöhen und auch durch die gewissenhafteste Auswahl deren, welche die Aufgabe haben, ihre Abgesandten im heiligen Lande zu sein. Fortschritt kann nur erzielt werden, wenn wir in diesem Zentrum unseres Glaubens die besten Typen christlicher Frömmigkeit, Gedankenarbeit, und Gelehrsamkeit vorweisen können.

VI. Ausbildung der Missionsarbeiter

I. Die Missionsgesellschaften sollen nur Männer und Frauen von erprobtem christlichen Charakter und christlicher Erfahrung in ihren Dienst berufen.

II. Sie haben von ihren leitenden Arbeitern eine biblisch-theologische und allgemeine Bildung zu fordern, die sie den Geistlichen der Kirche gleichstellt; dazu müssen sie ihnen eine Ausbildung geben, die sie so gründlich in das jüdische Geistesleben einführt, dass sie imstande sind, allen Juden ohne Unterschied das Evangelium in einer ihnen angemessenen Weise zu bringen. Andere Arbeiter, wie Kolporteure, usw., sollen eine Ausbildung empfangen, wie sie ihren besonderen Aufgaben entspricht.

III. Die Missionsgesellschaften sollen gemeinschaftlich bereits bestehende Institute zur Ausbildung von Missionsarbeitern im oben bezeichneten Sinne, wie das Institutum Judaicum Delitzschianum in Leipzig, unterstützen und ausbauen, und, wo sich die Notwendigkeit ergibt, neue Institute dieser Art schaffen und zwar möglichst in enger Verbindung mit Universitäten.

IV. Soll die Mission unter Israel geeignete Kräfte für ihr Werk gewinnen, so muss von den Kirchen erwartet werden, dass sie mehr Verständnis und Wertschätzung für die Arbeit und die Arbeiter dieser Mission zeigen und dass sie deren Aufgaben und Forderungen ihren Gliedern ans Herz legen.

(*a*) Besonders wichtig ist es, dass diese Aufgaben auch den Studenten der Theologie und anderen Studierenden nahegebracht werden, besonders aber durch Organisationen wie die christliche Studenten-Vereinigung in den verschiedenen Ländern.

(*b*) Auch sollte die Mission ihrerseits überall darauf bedacht sein, aus den Kreisen bewährter Judenchristen geeignete Arbeiter zu gewinnen und zu diesem Zwecke in engster Fühlung mit judenchristlichen Organisationen zu bleiben.

V. Die Mission soll für das leibliche und geistige Wohl ihrer Angestellten und Arbeiter durch ausreichende Besoldung, durch Gewährung von Urlaubszeiten und Möglichkeiten zur Fortbildung, sowie durch ihre Sicherstellung in Fällen der Invalidität und im Alter sorgen.

VII. Geistliche Kraefte

I. Die Konferenz tagte unter dem tiefen Eindruck von dem Reichtum ihrer Quellen, die sie in Gott hat durch Jesus Christus. Sie freut sich in der Erkenntnis, dass in dem fleischgewordenen Wort alle Fülle der Gottheit leibhaftig wohnt, und das alles, was die Arbeit in Seinem Reich irgend erfordert, durch das Innewohnen Seines Geistes zur Verfügung gestellt ist. Die Glieder der Konferenz erhoffen einmütig von Ihm eine neue Erfahrung von Seiner Liebe in Jesus Christus und von dem mächtigen Wirken Seines Geistes, und wollen sich demütig aufs neue in den Dienst der frohen Botschaft stellen.

II. Die Konferenz ist der Meinung, dass die Verkündigung der Christusbotschaft an die Juden, um wirksam zu sein, an die innere Kraft des Evangelisten die höchsten Anforderungen stellt, und dass die Kräftigung und Vertiefung des religiösen Lebens bei jedem Arbeiter von höchster Wichtigkeit ist. Und so möchte sie allen Nachdruck darauf legen, dass jede Mission an jeder ihrer Stationen ihr Werk so gestalten wolle, dass den Arbeitern für geregeltes Bibelstudium, Gebet und brüderliche Gemeinschaft die nötige Zeit gegeben wird. Sie ist davon überzeugt, dass selbst dann, wenn dadurch die Tätigkeit in einer Mission in ihrem Umfange beschränkt werden müsste, der innere Wert dieser Tätigkeit so bedeutend wüchse, dass das ganze Werk unermesslich an Kraft gewönne.

III. Die Konferenz ist der Meinung, dass die geistlichen Kräfte der Missionare in weitem Ausmasse von dem gesunden geistlichen Leben der aussendenden Missionsgesellschaft abhängen ; sie möchte daher die Missionen einladen, sich mit ihr zu vereinigen in rechter Busse für frühere Verfehlungen, in voller Hingabe an den Einfluss des Heiligen Geistes und in neuer Vertiefung in die geistlichen Schätze, die Gott im Alten wie im Neuen Testament niedergelegt hat, endlich auch im Reich der lebendigen Erfahrung der Kirche.

Die Konferenz möchte auf das bedeutsame Zeugnis

aufmerksam machen, das die missionarische Erfahrung von da und dort beibringt; wo nämlich Juden mit Ernst Christus angenommen haben, haben sie fast immer bezeugt, dass das, was sie zu Christus führte, vor allem das Leben treuer Jünger des Herrn oder eine Tat ihrer dienenden Liebe gewesen ist.

Im Hinblick auf die Verheissung: " Die auf den Herrn harren, kriegen neue Kraft, dass sie auffahren mit Flügeln wie Adler, dass sie laufen und nicht matt werden, dass sie wandeln und nicht müde werden," befiehlt die Konferenz ihre Teilnehmer und alle Arbeiter an dem Werk, die Juden für Christus zu gewinnen,—" Dem, der euch kann behüten ohne Fehler und stellen vor das Angesicht Seiner Herrlichkeit unsträflich mit Freuden."

VIII. Zusammenarbeit

Die Weltkonferenz möchte zunächst ihrer Freude Ausdruck geben über die fortschreitende Zusammenarbeit zwischen den verschiedenen christlichen Organisationen, die sich mit der Arbeit unter dem Volke Israel befassen. Diese Konferenz ist selbst das beste Beispiel dafür und beweist aufs neue und in überzeugender Weise die Notwendigkeit und den Wunsch nach einer umfassenderen und fruchtbareren Zusammenarbeit. Die Konferenz betont ferner, dass die ihr gebotenen grossen Möglichkeiten nur dann verwirklicht werden können, wenn ihre Arbeit und ihre Ziele vom lebendigen Interesse und der Arbeit der Kirchen getragen wird.

Die Konferenz hält es für sehr günstig, dass im Internationalen Missionsrat bereits eine Organisation besteht, die nicht nur diese Konferenz ermöglicht hat, sondern durch die auch die Vorschläge dieser Konferenz den verschiedenen Gesellschaften und den nationalen Missionsorganisationen mitgeteilt werden können zur Erwägung und weiteren Beschlussfassung.

I. Wir ersuchen daher den Internationalen Missionsrat bei seiner nächsten Tagung die Frage zu prüfen, wie er die in der Missionsarbeit stehenden verschiedenen Gesellschaften zu engerer Zusammenarbeit bringen kann, und wie die Arbeit unter den Juden einen zentraleren Platz unter den Aufgaben und der opferwilligen Dienstbereitschaft der Kirchen finden kann.

II. Wir möchten den Rat bitten, die Vorschläge und Empfehlungen der Konferenz den interessierten Kirchen und Organisationen bekanntzugeben und ebenso Vorkehrungen zu treffen, um eine dauernde Fühlung und gegenseitige Beratung unter den bestehenden Gesellschaften vorzubereiten und zu fördern, damit sie ihre Kenntnisse und Erfahrungen in den gemeinsamen Problemen gegenseitig austauschen, gemeinsame Nachforschungen und Studien machen können auf solchen Gebieten, auf denen gemeinsames Vorgehen wünschenswert ist und überhaupt zusammenarbeiten können, je nachdem dies von Zeit zu Zeit wünschenswert erscheint.

III. Angesichts der neuen Möglichkeiten für Ausdehnung der missionarischen Dienstleistung, auf die die Aufmerksamkeit der Konferenz gelenkt wurde, angesichts der Grösse und Schwierigkeit der zu lösenden Aufgabe, der beschränkten Arbeitskräfte und Geldmittel, empfiehlt die Konferenz dringend, alle nur verfügbaren Mittel sorgfältig zusammenzuhalten und zur Wirkung zu bringen. Dies kann dadurch erreicht werden, dass die verschiedenen Dienstleistungen nicht unnütz verdoppelt werden und das überhaupt eine Zersplitterung der Pläne und Unternehmungen vermieden wird.

IV. Die Konferenz ersucht den Internationalen Missionsrat, an den christlichen Studentweltbund, an das Welt komitee der christlichen Jünglings- und Frauenvereine, sowie an die Jugendorganisationen innerhalb der Kirchen eine Einladung zur Mitarbeit auf den verschiedenen Gebieten missionarischer Mitarbeit ergehen zu lassen.

VI. Bis zur Beschlussfassung durch den Internationalen Missionsrat empfiehlt die Konferenz, dass das Vorbereitungskomitee, so wie es durch den Geschäftsführenden Ausschuss zusammengestellt wird, bestehen bleibe, um etwaige notwendige Massnahmen in der Zwischenzeit treffen zu können.

IX. Frauen-Arbeit

I. Unter den sozialen Wandlungen, die in der heutigen Welt Platz gegriffen haben, ist nichts so völlig neugestaltet worden, wie die Stellung und der Wirkungskreis der Frauen. Im besonderen aber ist es die Judin, die nicht nur von dieser durch die Welt gehenden Bewegung, sondern auch von neuen Idealen und von dem Zerfall von Sitte und Herkommen innerhalb ihres eigenen Volkes beeinflusst wird. Die grössere gesellschaftliche Freiheit und die Entschränkung ihrer geistigen und seelischen Kräfte, machen die jüdischen Frauen zu einem neuen Zentrum von Kräften, die für das Gute oder Böse sich auswirken. Umso dringender tut es not, die Frauen dieser grossen Volksgemeinschaft in Berührung mit den geistlichen Kräften und den sittlichen Weisungen Jesu Christi zu bringen.

II. Wir empfehlen, dass christlichen Frauen diese Not ans Herz gelegt werde, und dass zum Gebrauch der in der Frauenmission stehenden Arbeiter Literatur ausgewählt oder neu verfasst werde, die sich mit dem jüdischen Volk und den zur Zeit unter ihnen herrschenden Zuständen befasse.

III. Es sollte dafür gesorgt werden, dass sich mehr Frauen diesem Dienst widmen und in Wort und Wandel Christus seinem Volke darstellen. Es sind Arbeiterinnen aller Art nötig: Bibelfrauen, Kranken- und Armenpflegerinnen, Aerztinnen, Lehrerinnen, Industrielehrerinnen, Leiterinnen von gesellschaftlichen Unternehmungen und von Hospizen.

IV. Säuglings- und andere Kliniken, Apotheken, Mütterberatungsstellen, Näh- und Abendkurse, Lesezimmer, Klubs und Studienkränzchen, Mütterfreizeiten, Dienstvermittlungen würden erwünschte Berührungspunkte bilden.

V. Für jüngere Mädchen in Industrie-, Handels- und Unterrichtszentren bringen wir Mädchenheime in Vorschlag, wie sie sich als dringendes Bedürfnis erwiesen haben. Für alle Dienste dieser Art sind Frauen von hoher Gesinnung und guter Vorbildung erforderlich.

VI. Wir betonen ausdrücklich, dass auf keinem Missionsfeld dieser Dienst an Frauen mit vollem Erfolg geübt werden kann, wenn nicht auch in den Missionsleitungen Frauen in entsprechender Zahl vertreten sind, die solchem Werk vorstehen, besonders in den Ausschüssen, die sich mit der Auswahl der Auszusendenden befassen.

VII. Wir empfehlen, dass geschulte, christliche Jüdinnen, wo immer möglich, im Dienste des Evangeliums an ihrem Volke verwendet werden, und das unter jüdisch-christlichen Frauen Missionsgruppen gebildet werden, die die ihnen Anvertrauten für das weltweite Missionsunternehmen anfeuern.

BESCHLÜSSE DER WARSCHAUER KONFERENZ

I. Evangelisation und Botschaft

Wir, die Tagung für Verkundigung der christlichen Botschaft an die Juden, wünschen hiermit dem jüdischen Volk unsere innere Anteilnahme und freundliche Gesinnung zu erklären. Wir beklagen die lange Zeit der Ungerechtigkeit und Misshandlung der Juden seitens der christlichen Völker. Wir erklären solch Verhalten für eine Verletzung der Lehre und des Geistes Christi und wir rufen die Kirchen und jeden einzelnen Christen aller Enden auf, der Ungerechtigkeit und der Misshandlung gegenüber den Juden zu wehren und ihnen vielmehr in Wort und Tat die Gesinnung unsers Herrn und Meisters Jesus Christus zu erweisen, der ihr und unser Heiland ist.

I. Wir sind der Ueberzeugung, dass die Kirche Christi in der Judenmission einer neuen Zeit entgegengeht. Die Zeichen der Zeit erwecken neue Hoffnung für die Zukunft.

(*a*) Offenkundig ist der wirtschaftliche und gesellschaftliche Fortschrift der Juden in nahezu allen Ländern. Das Ghetto ist langsam im Verschwinden.

(*b*) In den meisten Ländern zeigt sich ein Verlangen nach besserer Bildung, nicht wie die alte Synagoge sie bot, sondern wie sie die staatlichen Schulen gewähren.

(*c*) Es findet sich eine neue Einstellung gegenüber der grössten Tatsache der Geschichte, d.i. Jesus Christus.

(*d*) Neu erwacht ist das völkische Bewusstsein, wie es sich zeigt im Zionismus und anderen Bewegungen. Sie schliessen in sich ein die Ablehnung würdeloser Angleichung und halten fest an der grosesn, geschichtlichen Bestimmung des jüdischen Volkes.

(*e*) Doch können einige der neuen Entwicklungen im Judentum recht bedrohlich werden für die Welt, wofern sie nicht in christliche Bahnen geleitet werden.

Aus all diesen Gründen sind wir überzeugt, dass die Ausbreitung des Evangeliums unter den Juden eine zwingende Notwendigkeit ist. Ihrer fünfzehn und eine halbe Million lebt zerstreut unter Christen, eine Zerstreuung, die selber ein Ruf Gottes an die Kirche ist.

Die Grundlage und Rechtfertigung für die Missionsarbeit an den Juden ist vor Allem der besondere Auftrag unsers Herrn Jesus und seine Liebe zu ihnen. Dagegen steht es ausser Zweifel, dass die Unterlassung der Mission unter den Juden die Kirche der grossen, geistlichen Förderung berauben würde, die ihr durch die Begabung des jüdischen Volkes zufallen würde, und die gesamte Kirche zur geistigen Dürre verurteilen müsste.

II. Wir bringen den Juden die Frohbotschaft von der Liebe Gottes, uns geoffenbart in Jesus, der erschienen ist den Menschen, gekreuzigt, auferstanden und in die Herrlichkeit erhoben ist. Er ist die Erfüllung des Gesetzes, der Erlöser der Menschheit von Sünde und Tod, die Erfüllung auch der Hoffnungen, davon die Propheten geredet haben, der wahrhaftige Messias, das fleischgewordene Wort Gottes.

Jesus Christus ist der geistige Mittelpunkt, von dem allein die Juden eine geistige Belebung und eine völkische Errettung erwarten dürfen. Er allein ist der rechte Trost, den sie in ihren Nöten je und je ersehnten ; er allein das Band, das ihr auseinanderfallendes Volkstum einmal wieder zusammenschliessen kann. Das Reich Gottes, das er zu bringen gekommen war, ist der ideale Gesellschaftszustand, durch dessen Verkündigung, wenn sie in seinem Geist geschieht, die Menschheit ihre Vollendung erreichen kann.

Wir haben diese Frohbotschaft zu bringen mit festem Glauben und in treuer Hingabe, die versucht, die geistlichen Belange der Juden zu verstehen.

III. Die weite Verbreitung der Juden in vielen christlichen Ländern und ihr Wohnen innerhalb der Grenzen unserer Kirchspiele veranlasst uns hinzuweisen auf die hier von der Vorsehung gegebene Gelegenheit, das Evangelium unsern jüdischen Nachbarn zu verkünden. Vor allem seien die Pfarrer solcher Kirchspiele dringend gebeten, die Bedeutung der Judenmission, geübt durch Zeugnis und Vorbild der Gemeindeglieder, im Auge zu behalten, auch für Ausbildung und Besoldung von Missionsarbeitern unter dem nahewohnenden jüdischen Volke aus örtlichen Kirchenmitteln oder denen der kirchlichen Synoden, Sorge zu tragen.

IV. Bei unserer Verkündigung sollten wir nicht die sieben und eine halbe Million jüdischer Frauen und Mädchen und ihre besonderen Bedürfnisse übersehen.

Unter den orthodoxen Juden ist die jüdische Frau jahrhundertelang verurteilt gewesen zu einer untergeordneten Stellung in religiösen Dingen und demzufolge stark unwissend im Geistlichen, wenn man von dem Zeremoniendienst in der Religion absieht. Doch als Frau und Mutter übt sie starken Einfluss. Sie kann die Ursache werden zu einem aus Unwissenheit erwachsenen fanatischen Widerstand gegen die christliche Botschaft. Sie kann jedoch ebenso dem christlichen Einfluss freie Bahn schaffen, unter den sie vielleicht früher gekommen ist. Als höchstes Ideal muss der jüdischen Frauenwelt vorgehalten werden die Annahme Jesu und seine Nachfolge, wie sie die jüdischen Frauen ehedem übten, die ihm dienten und als erste seine Auferstehung verkündeten.

V. Wir möchten die Aufmerksamkeit hinlenken auf die besondere Notwendigkeit, doch auch auf die günstige Gelegenheit zur Verkündigung des Evangeliums bei den wohlunterrichteten und gebildeten Juden, Männern, sowohl als Frauen in den grossen Hochschul-Mittelpunkten. Abgetrennt von ihrem Vaterhause und der Synagoge fühlen sich diese Studenten im höchsten Masse verlassen und vereinsamt. Sie sind die Träger der Zukunft, und ihr Gemüt ist merkwürdig offen für neue Gedanken. So können sie leicht beeinflusst werden von einer geeigneten

Form christlicher Apologetik etwa in Gestalt von passendem Schrifttum, weit mehr freilich noch durch Bezeugung von Teilnahme und christlicher Hilfe allerlei Art.

VI. Letztlich verweisen wir noch auf die Entschliessung der Budapester Tagung, betreffend die Taufe. Wir billigen sie im Allgemeinen als eine verständige Aeusserung über diese äusserst schwierige Frage :—

" Wir machen auf die Tatsache aufmerksam, dass durch eine zu früh gewährt Taufe der getaufte Jude oft zu einem Aergernis für andere Juden wird und zu einem Vorwurf für die Mission und für die Kirche.

" Wenn ein Jude die Taufe verlangt, soll der Missionar sorgfältig den Ernst seines Wollens, sowie sein Leben prüfen, um gewiss zu sein, dass ihn keine abwegigen Beweggründe leiten.

" Das Ziel der Mission besteht nicht darin, Propaganda zu machen, sondern Seelen für Christus zu gewinnen und sie zu einem Leben in der Heiligung zu führen. Der Missionar soll daher eine besondere Vorsicht bei der Taufe dort anwenden, wo keine christliche Gemeinde den Bekehrten aufnimmt und ihm die notwendige geistliche Hilfe und Führung gibt. Der Taufe soll ein wohldurchdachter und sorgfältiger Unterricht vorangehen. Wo es möglich ist, wird ein genaues Taufregister geführt."

II. Missionsmethoden

I. Der Methoden, den Juden das Evangelium nahezubringen, sind viele. Es ist nicht möglich, ein bestimmtes Schema der Methoden aufzustellen, das für jedes Gebiet massgebend wäre—örtliche Bedürfnisse und Möglichkeiten haben da mitzusprechen. Das aber muss unbedingt betont werden,—

(*a*) dass nur solche Arbeit die beste Wirkung verspricht, die mit der ganzen Hingabe geheiligter Persönlichkeiten getrieben und vom Geiste Christi geleitet wird, der ein Geist der Wahrheit und der Liebe ist.

(*b*) Für die Predigt des Evangeliums und die Unterweisung in der christlichen Lehre bedarf es nicht blos fester Mittelpunkte in Kirchen und Versammlungsräumen, die zu diesem Zwecke sonderlich bestimmt sind, sondern auch öffentlicher Vorträge und Reisen im weiteren Umkreise zur Evangelisation unter Juden.

(*c*) Die persönliche Verkündigung des Evangeliums muss unterstützt werden durch eine Literatur, die auf die verschiedenen Gruppen der Juden Rücksicht nimmt, geschrieben in ihrer eigenen Sprache und in der Sprache des Landes, in dem sie wohnen. Für höher gebildete Juden empfiehlt es sich, die vorhandene christliche Literatur zu verwenden, die den Bedürfnissen der modernen Menschen entspricht. Daneben sollte auch für gute Literatur zur Aufklärung der Christen über unsere Aufgabe an den Juden gesorgt werden.

II. Wir möchten zur Berücksichtigung den Vorschlag der Budapester Konferenz empfehlen, dass dem Internationalen Missionsrat anheim gegeben werde, die Bildung von vier Komittees in die Wege zu leiten, die die Arbeit in Osteuropa, Mitteleuropa, Grossbritannien, und Nordamerika zu vertreten und unter Zuziehung eines Sekretärs des Internationalen Missionsrats für die Schaffung einer geeigneten Literatur zu sorgen hätten.

III. Es haben sich an verschiedenen Stellen des Arbeitsgebiets noch folgende Methoden als möglich und erfolgreich erwiesen :

(*a*) Unterricht und Erziehung,
(*b*) Aerztliche Stationen,
(*c*) Arbeitsstätten,
(*d*) Heime,
(*e*) Studentische Bibelkreise,
(*f*) Mitarbeit durch Gemeindepflege,
(*g*) Hausbesuche,
(*h*) Versammlungen unter freiem Himmel,
(*i*) Sommerlager.
(*j*) Lichtbilder, Radio u. a. Mittel,

das gesamte Leben der Juden durch das Evangelium zu beeinflussen.

Soweit diese Methoden Liebestätigkeit darstellen, muss alles vermieden werden, was die Empfänger demoralisieren könnte. Ebenso ist alles zu vermeiden, was den Eindruck erwecken könnte, als ob die Juden ihrer Volksgemeinschaft entzogen werden sollten. Welche Methoden immer auf einem bestimmten Arbeitsfelde für richtig befunden und angenommen werden, so gilt es, sie so wirksam wie möglich zu machen und auf bestimmte Zweige der Tätigkeit die Kraft möglichst zu konzentrieren.

III. Ausbildung der Missionsarbeiter

Die Judenmission steht heute vor gewaltigen Aufgaben. Der Mangel an geeigneten Arbeitern ist erschütterend. Daher ist die Gewinnung und Ausbildung von Zeugen Christi für Israel von entscheidender Bedeutung, und hinsichtlich dieses Gegenstandes wird Folgendes hervorgehoben :—

I. Was die Betätigung des Christen und des Judenchristen in der Judenmission betrifft—

(*a*) Von Natur eignet sich kein Mensch für die Arbeit im Reiche Gottes. Der Missionsarbeiter muss von der gläubigen Gemeinde erbeten, von Gott berufen, und zur Arbeit ausgerüstet und entsprechend vorbereitet sein. Die Verschiedenheiten der einzelnen Volks- und Religionsgruppen, die durch Geburt, Erziehung, Umwelt, durch das Geschlecht und die besondere persönliche Begabung bedingt sind, sind anzuerkennen. Es gibt, jedoch, keinen wesentlichen Unterschied zwischen den aus Juden und Nichtjuden stammenden Arbeitern. Beide sind eins in Christus. Die Hauptsache ist, dass der Missionsarbeiter eine christliche Persönlichkeit ist, die aus Leibe allen alles sein will.

(*b*) Deshalb eignen sich sowohl die Juden-, als auch die Nichtjuden-Christen für jede Art der Tätigkeit. Beide sind erwünscht und beide sind gleichberechtigt. Sie sollen einander ergänzen und mit den ihnen von Gott verliehenen Gaben dienen.

II. Eine gründliche biblisch-theologische und allgemeine Ausbildung wird vorausgesetzt, aber die veränderten Verhältnisse innerhalb des Judentums erfordern eine besondere Aufmerksamkeit auf Folgendes—

(*a*) Erlernung der hebräischen und jüdischen Sprache, wo die Verhältnisse es verlangen;

(*b*) Kenntnis der Theologie des Talmud, der Geschichte der Juden bis zur Gegenwart, der religiösen und nationalen Strömungen innerhalb des Judentums (Chassidismus, Reformjudentum, und Zionismus), und der neuesten jüdischen Literatur.

III. Hinsichts der Arten der Ausbildung—

1. (*a*) Die verschiedenen Berufsarbeiter, (und zwar Führer und Leiter, Missionare, Colporteure, Krankenschwestern, Bibelfrauen, usw.), bedürfen alle einer entsprechenden fachmässigen, sorgfältigen Ausbildung. Die Führer und Leiter sollen in der Regel darin den Pfarrern der Kirchen nicht nachstehen.

(*b*) Für Europa werden zwei Zentren der Ausbildung für nötig erachtet: für den Westen soll das bewährte Institutum Judaicum Delitzschianum in Leipzig, für den Osten die neugegründete Anstalt in Warschau gefördert und ausgebaut werden. Beide Anstalten stehen allen Gesellschaften und Kirchen offen. Aehnliche Anstalten sollen dort eröffnet werden, wo sie nötig sind.

(*c*) Um die Missionsarbeiter auf der Höhe zu erhalten und ihnen neue Anregungen zu geben, sollen von Zeit zu Zeit Fortbildungskurse veranstaltet werden.

2. (*a*) Um Freunde und freiwillige Mitarbeiter heranzubilden und in den Gemeinden lebendiges Interesse für Judenmission zu wecken, sollen besondere Missionskurse, Freizeiten, und Konferenzen für Pastoren, Lehrer, Evangelisten, und interessierte Gemeindemitglieder, eingerichtet werden.

(*b*) Um das Interesse und die Mithilfe der studierenden Jugend für die Judenmission zu erwecken und zu gewinnen, soll ein Aufruf an die christliche Jugendorganisationen gerichtet werden.

(*c*) Ein Handbuch für Judenmission—nach Art der Handbücher, die durch den Ausschuss für Vorbereitung zum Missionsberuf in New York hersausgegeben werden, und D. Dalman's Handbuch für Judenmission—soll allen, die sich mit Judenmission beschäftigen wollen, die erforderliche Handreichung bieten.

IV. Damit diese Ziele erreicht werden können, ist eine enge Zusammenarbeit der bestehenden Organisationen erforderlich.

IV. Die Besetzung des Missionsfeldes

Die jüdische Frage ist schon deshalb sehr schwierig, weil die Juden fast unter allen Völkern und in allen Lebensberufen zu finden sind. Trotzdem gibt es aber einen einheitlichen Lebenstypus, welcher darum auch unsererseits eine einheitliche Behandlung verlangt. Die Rolle, die das jüdische Volk spielt, geht weit über das hinaus, was die Zahl der Juden in der Welt voraussetzen lässt und zwar einesteils wegen ihrer regen Teilnahme an dem intellektuellen, geschäftlichen und politischen Leben in den Ländern, in denen sie wohnen, und andererseits infolge ihres Verhältnisses zu nicht-christlichen Geistesbewegungen und Richtungen, wie z.B. zu dem Mohammedanismus, usw.

Wenn man das Arbeitsfeld für Evangelisation unter den Juden überblickt, bemerkt man, dass grosse Gebiete wenig oder gar nicht besetzt sind, dazwischen aber einzelne Gegenden verhältnismässig mit Arbeitern überfüllt sind. Darum ist diese Konferenz der Meinung, dass eine Neuordnung der Missionstätigkeit dringend notwendig ist, wobei das Arbeitsfeld als Ganzes in Betracht gezogen werden muss und bei der die wichtigsten Arbeitszentren besonders berücksichtigt werden. Die Konferenz empfiehlt darum Folgendes :

I. Unbesetzte Arbeitsfelder wie diejenigen, welche man in Mittel-, Ost- und Südeuropa und in Südamerica findet, sollen unverzüglich und in besonderer Weise in Angriff genommen werden.

II. Wegen der Ausdehnung dieses Arbeitsfeldes und der daraus entstehenden Unmöglichkeit, dasselbe in der nächsten Zukunft genügend zu besetzen, empfiehlt die Konferenz, dass von gewissen wichtigen Zentren aus die Umgegend in Arbeit genommen werden sollte, und zwar nicht nur durch Kolporteure, sondern durch gehörig ausgebildete Reiseprediger.

III. Man soll den Tausenden von jüdischen Studenten an den Hochschulen und Universitäten der ganzen Welt besondere Beachtung widmen, weil sie von der christlichen Heilsbotschaft kaum noch berührt worden sind.

IV. Die Konferenz legt es den christlichen Kirchen des europäischen Festlandes dringend ans Herz, ihre besondere Verantwortlichkeit für die Evangelisationsarbeit unter den Juden, die bei ihnen wohnen, zu prüfen und ihr gerecht zu werden. Die Konferenz richtet auch an diejenigen evangelischen Kirchen, welche sich bisher für die Arbeit der Evangelisation der Juden nicht interessiert haben, die ernste Bitte, die gegenwärtige günstige Gelegenheit wahrzunehmen, und an dem Vorrecht und an der Verantwortung für dieses grosse und wichtige Werk teilzunehmen.

V. Der Internationale Missionsrat soll ersucht werden, eine Uebersicht über die Missionsfelder in Angriff zu nehmen, damit die Missionsgesellschaften eine Anleitung für geeignete Verteilung der Arbeit in der Zukunft haben.

V. Geistliche Kraefte

I. Die Konferenz ist sich tief bewusst, dass die geistlichen Kräfte die Hauptsache in der Arbeit der Mission unter den Juden bilden. Der Mangel an Kraft in der Vergangenheit kann auf Folgendes zurückgeführt werden :—

(*a*) Mangel an Interesse, Wärme und Gebet für die Judenmission innerhalb der Kirche. Wir danken Gott für allen bisherigen hingehenden Dienst in dieser Sache, aber wenn wir an die grossen Aufgaben, die durch die jetzige Lage gegeben sind, denken, sind wir uns dessen bewusst, dass unsere Arbeit in der Vergangenheit nicht immer recht erfasst, nicht weitsichtig geplant, und nicht mit ganzem Herzen unternommen worden ist. Das hat zweifellos Verlust an Kraft für unser Werk gebracht.

(*b*) Die Sünden der Christenheit den Juden gegenüber bekennen wir offen. Verfolgung, Unwissenheit und Gleichgültigkeit haben die Arbeit gehindert, Gelegenheiten vereitelt, offene Türen geschlossen, und Kraft vergeudet. Daher kam es, dass die Kirche oft nicht nach dem Sinn und Willen Jesu gehandelt und die Mittel, die Gott zur Verfügung stellte, nicht ausgenutzt hat.

(*c*) Das schlechte Beispiel, welches der Durchschnittschrist in seinem Leben und Umgang zeigte, hat die Entfaltung der erlösenden und segnenden Macht Jesu verhindert. Sowie das beste Argument für Jesum ein würdiges christliches Leben ist, also ist der grösste Feind geistlicher Kraft ein inkonsequentes Leben.

II. Die Konferenz ist sich bewusst und ist dankbar dafür, dass trotz aller Schwierigkeiten in der Judenmission, der Arbeiter seine innerste Befriedigung nicht in sich, sondern in Gott suchen muss. Dem auferstandenen Christus ist alle Macht gegeben im Himmel und auf Erden. Durch die Kraft seines lebengebenden Geistes kann er sich alle Dinge untertan machen. Er hat verheissen, bei seinen Dienern zu bleiben, bis an der Welt Ende, und seine Gegenwart wirkt Kraft und Leben.

III. Damit geistliche Kraft für uns und durch uns für die Welt wirksam werde, müssen wir die von Gott gegebenen Mittel benutzen.

1. Was die Pflege unseres inneren Lebens betrifft, kann nicht stark genug betont werden, dass alle geistliche Kraft uns nur zu Teil wird durch beständige Verbindung mit der Quelle der Kraft. Die Mittel hierzu liegen auf der Hand :— Ein regelmässiges Studium der heiligen Schrift, ein Leben des Gebetes und innerer Sammlung, Gottes Absichten mit seinem alten Bundesvolke nie aus dem Auge lassen, dem

Beispiel unseres Herrn, der Propheten und Apostel nachstrebend, und Gottes Verheissungen in zuversichtlichem Glauben erfassen. Dieser Glaube wird dem schweren Problem klar ins Auge sehen, Schwierigkeiten nicht verkleinern, aber er wird auch mit den Kräften rechnen, die auf unserer Seite sind, und wird glauben, dass wir alles vermögen durch Jesum Christum.

2. Gott will durch seine Knechte und Mägde geistliche Kräfte in anderen wirksam werden lassen. Die Methoden, durch welche geistliche Beeinflussung erreicht wird, sind schwer im Einzelnen zu bestimmen und aufzuzählen, aber die Konferenz schlägt nachstehende, als für den Erfolg ausschlaggebend, vor :—

(*a*) Ein dem Herrn geweihtes Leben als die beste Empfehlung für das Evangelium.

(*b*) Menschliche Geistesgaben und Herzensbildung, die dem Dienste Christi geweiht sind.

(*c*) Einen klaren Blick auf das Endziel aller unserer Tätigkeit, das heisst, Juden für Jesum Christum gewinnen.

(*d*) Im Hinblick auf die grossen Gefahren für das geistliche Leben, die der Vereinsamung drohen, wird empfohlen, das Beispiel unseres Herrn zu befolgen : Die Arbeiter je zwei und zwei auszusenden.

IV. Geistliche Kraft wird durch Trennung und Uneinigkeit vergeudet. Wir glauben, dass eine einheitliche Front eine Zunahme an Kraft bedeuten würde und dass, wenn mehr zusammengearbeitet und beraten würde, die Arbeit erfolgreicher und die Begeisterung grösser und mancher einsame Arbeiter durch den Segen christlicher Gemeinschaft ermuntert würde.

Wir glauben, dass mit Gottes Hilfe die unwiderstehlichen Kräfte, welche den Jüngern und Märtyrern der Apostelzeit gegeben waren und die Welt erneuerten, auch uns mitgeteilt werden können für unsere heutigen Bedürfnisse, und immer der siegreichen Verkündigung der apostolischen Botschaft des Gekreuzigten, Auferstandenen und lebenden Herrn folgen werden.

Endlich möchten die Glieder der Konferenz,—sich klar

bewusst, dass die Judenmission im Einklang mit dem ganzen Heilsplane Gottes steht,—alle diejenigen, welche in diesem grossen Werke stehen, dringend bitten, hoffnungsvoll und mutig fortzufahren, und sie legen sie Dem ans Herz, der überschwänglich tun kann über alles, das wir bitten oder verstehen, nach der Kraft, die in uns wirkt.

SPECIAL RESOLUTION OF BOTH CONFERENCES

International Hebrew Christian Alliance

The Conference has learned with great interest and sympathy of the formation and growth of the International Hebrew Christian Alliance, and expresses the hope that it may serve in uniting Christian Jews throughout the world in an enriching spiritual fellowship and become a blessing for the Jewish people as also for the Christian Church.

SONDERBESCHLUS DER KONFERENZEN

Internationale Judenchristliche Allianz

Die Konferenz hat mit grossem Interesse und Teilnahme von der Gründung und Entwickelung der Judenchristlichen Allianz gehört, und gibt der Hoffnung Ausdruck, dass diese Allianz dazu dienen möge, Juden-Christen in der ganzen Welt zu vereinigen und ihre geistige Gemeinschaft zu fördern, und dass die Allianz ein Segen werde für das jüdische Volk und für die christliche Kirche.

LIST OF CONFERENCE MEMBERS

CONFERENCE OFFICIALS

(Members of Both Conferences)

Chairman of Conferences

Dr John R. Mott, International Missionary Council, New York, U.S.A.

Chairman of Arrangements Committee

Rev. J. A. C. Mackellar, B.D., Church of Scotland, Glasgow, Scotland.

Secretaries

Mr Kenneth Maclennan, Conference of Missionary Societies, London, England.

Dr J. Macdonald Webster, United Free Church of Scotland, Edinburgh, Scotland.

Miss Janet B. Blake, United Free Church of Scotland, Edinburgh, Scotland.

MEMBERS OF BUDAPEST CONFERENCE

7th to 13th April 1927

Black, Rev. James M., D.D., United Free Church of Scotland Jewish Mission, Edinburgh, Scotland.

Bruce, Miss A. B., Church of Scotland W.A.J.M., Edinburgh, Scotland.

Beyer, Missionsinspektor Georg, Berlin Missionary Society, Berlin, Germany.

Brookman, Mr F. E., Open Brethren, Denver, Colo., U.S.A.

Brookman, Mrs F. E., Open Brethren, Denver, Colo., U.S.A.

Buist, Mr W. H., O.B.E., J.P., United Free Church of Scotland Jewish Mission, Dundee, Scotland.

Colligan, Rev. J. Hay, Presbyterian Church of England Jewish Mission, London, England.

CONNING, Rev. J. S., D.D., Presbyterian Church U.S.A., New York, N.Y., U.S.A.

CONNING, Mrs, Presbyterian Church U.S.A., New York, N.Y., U.S.A.

CSOPJÁK, Mr Attila, Hungarian Baptist Church, Kispest, Hungary.

EHRENBERG, Pfarrer Hans, D.Th., Prussian Evangelical Church, Bochum, Germany.

EINSPRUCH, Rev. Henry, United Lutheran Church, Baltimore, Md., U.S.A.

EXLEY, Rev. Frank J., British Jews Society, London, England.

FLIEDNER, Pfarrer Rudolf, West German Jewish Mission, Cologne, Germany.

FORGÁCS, Pastor Gyula, Hungarian Reformed Church, Sárospatak, Hungary.

FUNK, Pastor Martin, Methodist Episcopal Church in Hungary, Budapest, Hungary.

GÁNCS, Pastor, Hungarian Lutheran Church, Budapest, Hungary.

GARVIE, Rev. Principal A. E., D.D., Congregational Union, London, England.

GERHARDT, Missionsdirektor August, Basel Jewish Mission, Basel, Switzerland.

GERWICH, Pastor Georg, Hungarian Baptist Church, Budapest, Hungary.

GILL, Rev. C. H., Church Missions to Jews, London, England.

GOULD, Rev. Canon S., D.D., Church of England in Canada, Toronto, Canada.

GREENBAUM, Rev. E. S., Hebrew Christian Alliance, Newark, N.J., U.S.A.

GREENBERG, Rev. H. G., Church of England in New York, New York, N.Y., U.S.A.

HAMMOND, Miss M., Church Missions to Jews, London, England.

HARLING, Pastor Otto von, Institutum Judaicum Delitzschianum, Leipzig, Germany.

HEISTAD, Miss Anna, Methodist Episcopal Church, Chicago, Ill., U.S.A.

IHLEN, Rev. Professor Chr., D.Th., Norwegian Israelsmission, Oslo, Norway.

JEREMIAS, Rev. Professor Alfred, D.Th., Leipzig Jewish Mission, Leipzig, Germany.

KAMMEYER, Rev. K. H., Dutch Society for Israel, Amsterdam, Holland.

KELLER, Rev. Adolf, D.Th., Swiss Protestant Federation, Zurich, Switzerland.

KESSLER, Generalsuperintendent Hans, D.Th., Berlin Jewish Mission, Berlin, Germany.

LEVISON, Sir Leon, International Hebrew Christian Alliance, Edinburgh, Scotland.

LOWRIE, Mr Donald, Student Christian Movement, Prague, Czecho-Slovakia.

LUNDAHL, Rev. J. E., Northern Missionary Council, Stockholm, Sweden.

M'EWEN, Mrs, United Free Church of Scotland W.J.M., Edinburgh, Scotland.

MACINNES, Right Rev. Bishop Rennie, D.D., represented by Rev. Canon Herbert Danby, D.D., Jerusalem and the East Mission, Jerusalem, Palestine.

M'LEISH, Rev. A., United Free Church of Scotland Mission, Ajmer, India.

MACLENNAN, Mrs Kenneth, London, England.

MADISON, Mr W. N., International Missionary Council, New York, N.Y., U.S.A.

MATHEWS, Mr Basil, World's Committee Y.M.C.A., Geneva, Switzerland.

MATHEWS, MRS, Geneva, Switzerland.

MILLER, Mr Francis P., World Student Christian Federation, Geneva, Switzerland.

NES, Rev. J. van, Reformed Churches of the Netherlands, The Hague, Holland.

NEWGEWIRTZ, Rev. D. J., Church of England in Canada, Montreal, Canada.

NICHOLSON, Bishop Thomas, D.D., Methodist Episcopal Church, Detroit, Mich., U.S.A.

Nicholson, Mrs, Methodist Episcopal Church, Detroit, Mich., U.S.A.

Nuelsen, Bishop John L., D.D., Methodist Episcopal Church, Zurich, Switzerland.

Nuelsen, Mrs, Methodist Episcopal Church, Zurich, Switzerland.

Pap, Rev. Professor Bilkei, Hungarian Reformed Church, Budapest, Hungary.

Paul, Rev. Principal F. J., D.D., Presbyterian Church in Ireland Jewish Mission, Belfast, Ireland.

Pellmann, Pfarrer Karl, West German Jewish Mission, Essen, Germany.

Philcox, Mr H. N., British Jews Society, London, England.

Podmaniczky, Pastor the Baron Paul, Hungarian Lutheran Church, Budapest, Hungary.

Prudký, Pastor Francis, Evangelical Church of Czech Brethren, Olomouc, Czecho-Slovakia.

Ravasz, Right Rev. Bishop Ladislaus, Ph.D., Hungarian Reformed Church, Budapest, Hungary.

Ritson, Rev. John H., D.D., British and Foreign Bible Society, London, England.

Rottenberg, Rev. John, Hebrew Christian Testimony to Israel, London, England.

Rouse, Miss Ruth, Church of England Missionary Council, London, England.

Staerk, Rev. Professor Willy, D.Th., The University, Jena, Germany.

Stenberg, Pastor Hj., Swedish Israelsmission, Stockholm, Sweden.

Stewart, Rev. Alex., D.D., Free Church of Scotland Foreign Mission, Edinburgh, Scotland.

Strahan, Miss R. E., Church Missions to Jews, Ballater, Scotland.

Szeberényi, Pastor D., Hungarian Lutheran Church, Budapest, Hungary.

Torm, Rev. Professor Frederick, D.D., The University, Copenhagen, Denmark.

Ulich, Pfarrer, Berlin Jewish Mission, Berlin, Germany.

VICTOR, Rev. Professor John, Ph.D., Hungarian Reformed Church, Budapest, Hungary.

WILKINSON, Rev. Samuel H., Mildmay Mission to the Jews, London, England.

WRONG, Miss, Student Christian Movement, London, England.

ZWERNEMANN, Superintendent G., D.D., Austrian Reformed Church, Vienna, Austria.

Missionary Members

ADENEY, Rev. J. Howard, Church Missions to Jews, Bucarest, Rumania.

BEVERIDGE, Rev. William, United Free Church of Scotland Mission, Budapest, Hungary.

BOYD, Miss, Church Missions to Jews, Bucarest, Rumania.

CHISHOLM, Rev. R. F., United Free Church of Scotland and Presbyterian Church of England Jewish Missions, Cluj-Kolozsvár, Rumania.

FEINSILBER, Mr Robert, Hebrew Christian Testimony to Israel, Budapest, Hungary.

FRANK, Rev. Arnold, D.D., Irish Presbyterian Mission, Hamburg, Germany.

GLUCKMAN, Mr Michael, Norwegian Israelsmission, Sofia, Bulgaria.

GOLDSTEIN, Dr John, Mildmay Mission to the Jews, Salonika, Greece.

HABERL, Professor Johannes, D.D., Swedish Israelsmission, Vienna, Austria.

HELLMANN, Miss Martha, Swedish Israelsmission, Vienna, Austria.

JOHNSON, Rev. Gisle C. T., Norwegian Israelsmission, Budapest, Hungary.

KARLSSON, Miss Anna, Swedish Israelsmission, Vienna, Austria.

KING, Rev. Alex., United Free Church of Scotland Mission, Budapest, Hungary.

LEITCH, Miss E. M., United Free Church of Scotland Mission, Budapest, Hungary.

LÖWY, Mr D. A., West German Jewish Mission, Cologne, Germany.

NAGY, Rev. Alex., Ph.D., United Free Church of Scotland Mission, Budapest, Hungary.

PRÉM, Miss Margit, United Free Church of Scotland Mission, Budapest, Hungary.

ROHOLD, Rev. S. B., British Jews Society, Haifa, Palestine.

RUDNITZKY, Rev. N., Oelberg Mission, Potsdam, Germany.

ZWEMER, Rev. Samuel M., D.D., Reformed Church in America, Cairo, Egypt.

MEMBERS OF WARSAW CONFERENCE

19*th to* 25*th April* 1927

D'AUBIGNÉ, Rev. Ch. Merle, D.D., French Protestant Federation, Paris, France.

BLACK, Rev. James M., D.D., United Free Church of Scotland Jewish Mission, Edinburgh, Scotland.

BEYER, Missionsinspektor Georg, Berlin Missionary Society, Berlin, Germany.

BIELING, Superintendent R., D.Th., Prussian Evangelical Church, Soldin, Germany.

BOOM, Rev. W. ten, Dutch Society for Israel, Hilversum, Holland.

BROOKMAN, Mr F. E., Open Brethren, Denver, Colo., U.S.A.

BROOKMAN, Mrs F. E., Open Brethren, Denver, Colo., U.S.A.

BUIST, Mr W. H., O.B.E., J.P., United Free Church of Scotland Jewish Mission, Dundee, Scotland.

BURSCHE, Rev. Juljusz, D.Th., Generalsuperintendent, Evangelical Church of Poland, Warsaw, Poland.

COLLIGAN, Rev. J. Hay, Presbyterian Church of England Jewish Mission, London, England.

CONNING, Rev. J. S., D.D., Presbyterian Church U.S.A., New York, N.Y., U.S.A.

CONNING, Mrs, Presbyterian Church U.S.A., New York, N.Y., U.S.A.

Davidson, Rev. I. E., International Hebrew Christian Alliance, London, England.

Deloff, Mr August, Reformed Church of Poland, Warsaw, Poland.

Dietrich, Pastor J., Evangelical Church of Poland, Lodz, Poland.

Einspruch, Rev. Henry, United Lutheran Church, Baltimore, Md., U.S.A.

Enholc, Mr Alex., British and Foreign Bible Society, Warsaw, Poland.

Exley, Rev. Frank J., British Jews Society, London, England.

Fauerholdt, Pastor I. V. R., Danish Israelsmission, Als, Denmark.

Garvie, Rev. Principal A. E., D.D., Congregational Union, London, England.

Gerhardt, Missionsdirektor August, Basel Jewish Mission, Basel, Switzerland.

Gill, Rev. C. H., Church Missions to Jews, London, England.

Gould, Rev. Canon S., D.D., Church of England in Canada, Toronto, Canada.

Greenbaum, Rev. E. S., Hebrew Christian Alliance, Newark, N.J., U.S.A.

Greenberg, Rev. H. G., Church of England in New York, New York, N.Y., U.S.A.

Haenisch, Mr Gerhard, United Evangelical Church in Poland, Poznań, Poland.

Hammond, Miss M., Church Missions to Jews, London, England.

Harling, Pastor Otto von, Institutum Judaicum Delitzschianum, Leipzig, Germany.

Harris, Mr Henry, Society of Friends, Warsaw, Poland.

Heistad, Miss Anna, Methodist Episcopal Church, Chicago, Ill., U.S.A.

Jeremias, Rev. Professor Alfred, D.Th., Leipzig Jewish Mission, Leipzig, Germany.

Johnson, Rev. Gisle C. T., Norwegian Israelsmission, Budapest, Hungary.

KRAFT, Pfarrer Alfred, Berlin Jewish Mission, Zaborze, Germany.

LADENBERGER, Pfarrer E. O., Evangelical Church A. and H. in Poland, Stryj, Poland.

LEVISON, Sir Leon, International Hebrew Christian Alliance, Edinburgh, Scotland.

LUNDAHL, Rev. J. E., Northern Missionary Council, Stockholm, Sweden.

M'EWEN, Mrs, United Free Church of Scotland W.J.M., Edinburgh, Scotland.

MACINNES, Right Rev. Bishop Rennie, D.D., represented by Rev. Canon Herbert Danby, D.D., Jerusalem and the East Mission, Jerusalem, Palestine.

MACLENNAN, Mrs Kenneth, London.

MADISON, Mr W. N., International Missionary Council, New York, N.Y., U.S.A.

MARTSINKOVSKY, Mr W., World Student Christian Federation, Prague, Czecho-Slovakia.

MATHESON, Rev. W. S., United Free Church of Scotland, Galashiels, Scotland.

NES, Rev. J. van, Reformed Churches of the Netherlands, The Hague, Holland.

NEUDING, Rev. John, Methodist Episcopal Church, Warsaw, Poland.

NEWGEWIRTZ, Rev. D. J., Church of England in Canada, Montreal, Canada.

PASZKO, Colonel Richard, Chaplain-General (Lutheran), Warsaw, Poland.

PAUL, Rev. Principal F. J., D.D., Presbyterian Church in Ireland Jewish Mission, Belfast, Ireland.

PHILCOX, Mr H. N., British Jews Society, London, England.

RASMUSSEN, Rev. J., Superintendent, Methodist Episcopal Church, Danzig.

SAARISALO, Pastor A., Finnish Missionary Society, Helsingfors, Finland.

SEMADENI, Rev. Wladislaw, Superintendent, Reformed Church of Poland, Warsaw, Poland.

SHAND, Miss A. S. H., Church of Scotland W.A.J.M., Edinburgh, Scotland.

STENBERG, Pastor Hj., Swedish Israelsmission, Stockholm, Sweden.

STEWART, Rev. Alex., D.D., Free Church of Scotland Foreign Mission, Edinburgh, Scotland.

SZERUDA, Rev. Professor John, Evangelical Church of Poland, Warsaw, Poland.

THORPE, Rev. A. St John, Church Missions to Jews, Beckenham, England.

THORPE, Mrs St John, Church Missions to Jews, Beckenham, England.

WEISENSTEIN, Mr W., West German Jewish Mission, Cologne, Germany.

WILES, Mr J. W., British and Foreign Bible Society, Belgrade, Jugo-Slavia.

WILKINSON, Rev. Samuel H., Mildmay Mission to the Jews, London, England.

ZIRKWITZ, Pastor Theodor, Evangelical Church of Poland, Bialystok, Poland.

Missionary Members

AJZEMAN, Mr Abraham, Church Missions to Jews, Lwów, Poland.

CARPENTER, Rev. H. C., Church Missions to Jews, Warsaw, Poland.

CHISHOLM, Rev. R. F., United Free Church of Scotland and Presbyterian Church of England Jewish Missions, Cluj-Kolozsvár, Rumania.

DOLMAN, Rev. George, Church Missions to Jews, Wandsbek, Germany.

FLAD, Rev. C. F. W., Church Missions to Jews (Abyssinia), St Légier, Switzerland.

FRANK, Rev. Arnold, D.D., Irish Presbyterian Mission, Hamburg, Germany.

FROHWEIN, Miss Hildegard, Basel Jewish Mission, Wilno, Poland.

GORODISHZ, Mr Peter, Barbican Mission, Bialystok, Poland.

KEITH, Miss M., Church Missions to Jews, Warsaw, Poland.

LANDSMAN, Rev. J. I., Church Missions to Jews, Warsaw, Poland.

NIELSEN, Miss Ingeborg, Danish Israelsmission, Lwów, Poland.

PANKHURST, Miss D. L., Church Missions to Jews, Warsaw, Poland.

RAD, Mr Paul, Irish Presbyterian Jewish Mission, Danzig.
ROHOLD, Rev. S. B., British Jews Society, Haifa, Palestine.
ROSENBAUM, Mr B., Basel Jewish Mission, Wilno, Poland.

SCHWEIZER, Mr L., Basel Jewish Mission, Lodz, Poland.
SILBERSTEIN, Mr J., Mildmay Mission to the Jews, Warsaw, Poland.
SPALENICE, Mr Max, British Jews Society, Cracow, Poland.

WOLF, Mr Edward, Basel Jewish Mission, Lodz, Poland.

ZWEMER, Rev. Samuel M., D.D., Reformed Church in America, Cairo, Egypt.

APPENDICES

A.—ANSWERS TO QUESTIONNAIRE

I. JEWISH POPULATIONS

ANY estimate of the Jewish population of the world can at best be only approximate, since most countries take no account of religion in their official census. For others only computations can be made. Many correspondents, to whom inquiries were addressed, are indefinite in their figures, and it is apparent that some have not yet become acquainted with the post-war geographical configuration of Europe. For example, the figures given by several correspondents for the same country vary by as much as two and a quarter millions. But all the information supplied has been sifted and checked, and then compared with statistics which appear in Jewish publications. As a result, the approximate Jewish population of the world may be set forth as follows :—

EUROPE	
British Isles	310,000
Holland	110,000
Belgium	50,000
France	155,000
Spain and Portugal	4,500
Italy	72,000
Switzerland	21,000
Denmark	5,500
Norway	1,500
Sweden	6,500
Finland	2,000
Germany	550,000
Czecho-Slovakia	360,000
Austria	350,000
Hungary	500,000
Jugo-Slavia	65,000
Bulgaria	40,000
Greece	88,500
Turkey	90,000
Rumania	950,000
Ukrainia	2,375,000
Russia	685,000
Poland	2,870,000
Baltic States, etc.	460,000
	10,121,500

AMERICA	
U.S.A.	3,750,000
Canada	160,000
Central America	17,000
West Indies	6,000
Argentine	145,000
Other S. American countries	7,500
	4,085,500

ASIA	
Turkey	78,000
Syria	40,000
Palestine	160,000
Arabia	25,000
Irak	87,500
Persia	50,000
India	41,500
Russia	100,000
China	1,000
Japan	2,000
Other parts	160,000
	745,000

AFRICA		AUSTRALASIA	
North African Lands .	258,000	Australia . . .	21,500
Egypt . . .	55,000	New Zealand . .	2,400
Abyssinia . .	80,000	Pacific Islands . .	1,600
East, Central and South Africa . .	64,500		
	457,500		25,500

SUMMARY

Europe . .	10,121,500
America . .	4,085,500
Asia . .	745,000
Africa . .	457,500
Australasia . .	25,500
Total . .	15,435,000

Inquiries have not elicited for any country what proportion of its Jews is employed in any particular occupation. It is, however, apparent that there is scarcely any pursuit in life without its Jewish representatives. In Tunisia we find Jews among the rag and bone collectors; Persia has its Jewish scavengers; in India Jews are found among the ordinary coolies; Rumania has its Jewish tinkers; in several East European countries many Jews are cab-drivers, and in almost all lands where they reside, they form a considerable section of the pedlars. In Middle and Eastern Europe, in Greece, Abyssinia, Great Britain, and America, they constitute a proportion of the artisan class; numbers are employed on railways, in transport work generally, in the public services, in clerking and kindred pursuits. Belgium seems to have its Jewish coal-miners as well as its diamond-cutters. Holland has likewise its diamond-cutters among the Jews, but there, and in Czecho-Slovakia, Hungary, etc., considerable numbers are dealers in cattle and farm produce. America, Germany, Sweden, Russia, Palestine, have their Jewish agriculturalists. In several lands—North America, Britain, Austria, Hungary, and elsewhere—very many are employed in tailoring; the ready-made clothing and furniture industries seem to be falling more and more into Jewish hands, as is also the fur industry. Among the bootleggers of America are many Jews; in some of the European and Asiatic countries the drink trade is largely in the hands of Jews, and they engage in catering, in hotel and tavern-keeping. In America radio has become to a great extent a Jewish business, and there as well as in some other lands the same applies to the cinema. Large numbers of Jews are also found in the theatrical and musical professions. Almost everywhere Jews are engaged as commission agents and middlemen, in betting concerns, money-lending, money-changing, in the jewelry business, in gold and silver working, in trade and commerce generally. Their interests in heavy industries have greatly increased in recent years, while in almost all lands the number engaged in the liberal professions—banking, medicine, law, journalism, teaching, engineering, dentistry, chemistry, etc.—is out of all proportion to their total numbers.

As it is expected that special statements will be submitted to the Conferences in regard to the distribution of missionary agents among these Jews and about their various methods of work, it is unnecessary to treat of these subjects here. It may, however, be noted generally that the Protestant Churches of those European lands (Poland, the Baltic States, Austria, Czecho-Slovakia, Hungary, Rumania), in which larger masses of Jews reside, take no definite or active share in Jewish evangelisation, although some of them are sympathetic and some of the ministers and clergy show a practical interest in it and in Missions established amongst them by foreign Churches and Societies. It is somewhat different in Germany where the Protestant Churches give financial support to three indigenous Jewish Mission Boards. Something similar, although in a lesser degree, is to be found in Holland, South Africa, and Australia. The Protestant Churches of Switzerland, and of the Northern European countries support Societies for Jewish Mission work in their own and other lands, but in Belgium, France, and Italy, the Protestants seem to make no effort to bring the Gospel to the Jews even of their own lands. In Great Britain and Ireland several Societies, including the largest Jewish Missionary organisation in the world, derive their support for work at home and abroad from the Anglican Church; the larger Presbyterian Churches have their own Jewish Mission Boards, directly appointed by the General Assemblies; but the Free Churches of England have no organisation for Jewish evangelisation, although many of their congregations contribute to the support of certain Societies. In recent years the sense of responsibility for evangelising the Jews of Canada and the United States has greatly increased in several of the Protestant Churches of these lands; some of the Churches there have created Jewish Mission Boards of their own, and generous support has also been rendered to various Societies.

In the United States the Roman Catholics have started work among Jews, and in Europe a Roman Catholic "Society of Friends of Israel" has been formed. Among its members are already seven Cardinals, fifty Archbishops, and a large number of priests. Jewish pupils are frequently found in Roman Catholic schools. There is no evidence that the Greek Orthodox Church takes any interest in Jewish Evangelisation.

II. THE PRESENT SITUATION IN JEWRY

As was to be expected, answers to the Questionnaire show that the Jewish people have been profoundly affected by the upheaval and the political changes of recent years. This is particularly true of the great Jewish areas of Europe, but there are reactions in other and distant lands. Owing to the new political configuration of the Old World, large numbers of Jews are under new State authorities, and, by immigration from Eastern Europe, countries which were neutral during the War, as well as most of the belligerent nations, have received additions to their Jewish populations. In broad outline, it may be said that Jews the world throughout have now political freedom and rights of citizenship, whereas in 1914 it is doubtful if even half their total number enjoyed or could claim such liberties, although in Sweden, for example, they cannot yet become members of the Cabinet, while in Rumania they are not accepted in the public services, nor as officers in the army.

At the same time, there has been a widespread increase of Anti-Semitism. In France only does it seem to have abated. In India, Australia, New Zealand, and Canada it is practically unknown. Evidences of it are seen in Switzerland, Holland, the Scandinavian lands, and Persia, but it is no more than sporadic. In Belgium, Greece, and the North African countries, it is not an open force. But in Middle and Eastern Europe generally it has developed greatly, and in such countries as Egypt, Palestine, Hungary, England, the United States of America, South Africa, Japan, where it was unknown before, strong Anti-Semitic tendencies are at work. In Rumania, there is a definitely Anti-Semitic party in Parliament. Writers indicate, in the main, very much the same causes for the present-day Anti-Semitic wave—racial differences, Jewish exclusiveness and success in business, the adoption by (some or many) Jews of Socialistic or Communistic views, and, in Palestine—in addition to these factors—the transfer of land.

On the religious side, from country after country it is reported that the majority of educated Jews have turned to agnosticism or atheism. Religious apathy or indifference grows apace, morals have suffered in many parts since the War, decadence is apparent almost everywhere, even in Palestine old-fashioned Orthodoxy is being rapidly undermined, materialism gains ground rapidly, and already drift from Judaism and the Synagogue has set in. It is stated that in America 80 per cent of the Jews are outside the Synagogue, while in the city of Berlin approximately 65 per cent have given up Judaism, and in many other large cities similar lapsing is seen, although the ratio may not be so high. Younger people in particular seem to have less and less regard for the tenets of their traditional faith and seek stimulus in Socialism and Labour Movements. A considerable number in America has turned to "Christian Science," in Hungary to Theosophy and Spiritualism, in many lands to Zionism and Nationalism. Indeed, with no small proportion of Jews, Zionism and Nationalism are taking the place of religious faith.

To what extent the Jewish National Movement has spread is not apparent, but Zionism is undoubtedly a force in the life of Jewry to-day. It is, however, not so deeply rooted as is sometimes assumed, although in some areas its influence expands. But it has little hold in countries like Germany, Czecho-Slovakia, Hungary, Greece, Denmark, Norway, Sweden, Finland, Egypt and the North African lands, Persia, etc. It is strong in Rumania, but even in Poland it is doubtful if half the Jews are Zionists. It is stated that practically all the Jews of South Africa and North America are Zionists, but their Zionism must be generally of a very theoretic type, as it is in many parts elsewhere. With very many who are reckoned as Zionists, the whole attachment to the movement seems to consist in the payment of a contribution, much as if it were merely a deserving charity. It is doubtful wisdom to accept at face value the highly coloured statements of Zionist publications. The majority of Liberal Jews in Europe appear to be opposed on principle both to Zionism and to Jewish Nationalism.

For the Christian missionary these changes and tendencies appear to be in certain respects a hindrance and in others an encouragement. Too often drift from the Synagogue is drift from religion, and increasing materialism has a like result. Anti-Semitism defeats its own ends and knits Jews more closely together. The new race consciousness, Zionism, and Nationalism tend to bring about a similar effect. Thus, if the old Ghetto is breaking up, new forces are set against the missionary. Zionists and Nationalists generally oppose Christian missions, less perhaps on religious grounds than for the reason that they denationalise the people. This fact in itself seems to point to the need for the Church and her missionary agency to restudy their enterprise and their method of shepherding converts.

That a new spirit of inquiry is, however, abroad need not be doubted. It would be too much to say that the majority of Jews are ready to accept the Gospel, but there is no question that very large numbers of them now show an open-mindedness heretofore unknown. The breakaway from Rabbinism and Talmudical influence, together with the freer conditions under which so many are now living, seem to dispose many to inquire into things and therefore also into the claims of Christianity. From many parts it is reported that there is to-day a willingness on the part of Jews to listen to the Christian missionary. From several countries we have it stated that there has been a decline of fanatical opposition. In Poland to-day, as well as in certain other parts of Europe, and in cities like Glasgow, it is relatively easy to get a large audience of Jews to hear addresses on the Christian Message. In North America also the Community Centres, opened by certain of the Churches, are drawing in larger numbers of Jews, who are said to be more approachable than in the past. All this indicates new and great opportunities for Christian missions, and it is lamented, particularly in

Eastern Europe, that the workers are far too few to meet the developing situation. But it may not be forgotten that the Synagogue, or official Judaism as such, still does its utmost to create hindrances, and in London an effort is being made to organise direct opposition to missionary work.

It may be observed that, while in several countries there are certain legal restrictions in regard to the age at which people may change their faith, nowhere do Government authorities seem to raise any difficulties about the conduct of Jewish Mission enterprise.

III. THE CHRISTIAN MESSAGE GENERALLY

Christianity claims to be the final and absolute religion, not only through the unique revelation given by Jesus Christ, but through its possession of the Holy Spirit guiding it into all truth. But it is not final and absolute in its expression of the whole truth in any particular age. Different facets of the truth as it is in Christ Jesus have flashed upon the world at different times. In the early centuries the Person of Jesus Christ held the thought of men ; at one time His Divinity, at another, His humanity coming into prominence. The contemplative and mystical elements of the faith were cultivated in cloister and nunnery of the Middle Ages. Justification by faith was the slogan of the Reformation, and the soul's progress to salvation through the reception of Divine grace roused the Reformers to a passionate declaration against a salvation by works. The Great Commission to go into all the world preaching the Gospel awakened the Church of the nineteenth century to its splendid missionary endeavours, and the impulse of the Gospel of love rousing sympathy and the spirit of helpfulness towards the poor and needy has created the ameliorative agencies of modern Christianity.

The Christian message is adequate for all the needs of men and for the needs of all men of every nation and age, if only the proper supplies are drawn from the unsearchable riches of Christ to meet these needs. From time to time the emphasis is changed, but the Message is the same —the assurance of forgiveness and a new life, within the wonderful fellowship of Christ—loving souls and a glorious hope for the future in the ever challenging vision of the Kingdom of God. On what aspect of the Christian Gospel must the emphasis be laid to-day in an approach to the Jew? What are the special religious circumstances and spiritual needs we have to meet? How can a sympathetic understanding between him and us be set up?

That is the question that is attempted to be answered in this section. The answers have not furnished much information of value. Possibly some of the questions were not sufficiently explicit. That may be why several of them were left unanswered and some of the writers missed the purport of others. Nevertheless, a few items of interest and value may be culled.

On the question how far and in what way Jews find help and consolation in their religion there is considerable diversity of opinion. Some assert they find no consolation. Others hold the view that they have a certain satisfaction in maintaining the faith of their fathers, and still others hold that the fulfilment of the laws which relate more intimately to family and social life does provide a measure of help and comfort to the orthodox pious Jew whose memory and imagination are quickened by the celebration of the great festival days. This veneration for the past and the comfort from the former days are mostly seen in the case of the older Jews—the younger generation treating their religious duties more lightly. It is noted that the sense of personal sin and the need of personal forgiveness are not acutely felt, and "one of the most difficult and important tasks of Christian missions is to awaken this sense."

To those elements of Jewish faith that minister comfort and help, it is obvious that the Christian worker should show appreciation and sympathy. He must necessarily combat any idea of self-righteousness or self-deception, but he is afforded an opportunity of "explaining the Jew to himself," bringing into prominence the blessings and truth of God the Jew possesses for the benefit of all and how these are perfected in Jesus Christ. The religion of the New Testament is the necessary completion of the Old Testament religion and "not a foreign growth as rabbinic Judaism is."

Many of the writers emphasise the importance of a true Christian life, abounding in charity and sympathy, leading to visitation of the poor and sick and the immense value of "a discreet and tactful" personal testimony to the power of Christ's salvation.

So many Jews, by their drift from the Synagogue and by their developing new forms of Judaism, express dissatisfaction with their religion, that it is asked if this provides a special opportunity for Christian missions. The evidence of the various workers is that it does. In many cases the discontented Jews seek to find satisfaction in "something new"; in America they turn to Christian Science, Theosophy, Spiritualism; in Europe, to Communism and Bolshevism. Many have openly thrown religion over and give themselves up to materialism and atheism, some making ridicule of all religion. The agnostic attitude is popular with many of the younger Jews. There are, however, many earnest-minded searchers after truth who have felt the difficulty of reconciling their religion with modern knowledge and they are ready to discuss the claims of Christianity. These deplore the methods of Christian missions in seeking to influence the most ignorant classes. From many fields reports of increased numbers of inquirers are received, and by nearly all the writers attention is called to the drifting of the young people from the Synagogue. This seems to serve as an excellent field for missionary service, so one writer advises "concentrate upon the young people." The liberalising tendencies of Reform Judaism also provide opportunity for the discussion of religious subjects in a freer atmosphere, one worker hoping that Reform Judaism may be made the stepping stone to a higher faith, and the circulation of the New Testament Scriptures and of suitable missionary literature is commended.

But there are manifest hindrances to the acceptance of the Christian message by the Jew, and these are grouped in the Questionnaire into moral, intellectual, social and political. The bulk of the writers add a fifth—religious, and it is on this that the chief stress is laid. Under this head are included—misunderstanding of the Old Testament, the dogmatic stringency of the Christian system of belief, the Trinity, the Birth, Incarnation and Deity of Christ, the predominance of supernaturalism and the historic revelation in Christ.

(*a*) *Moral Hindrances.*—The higher moral standard of Christianity acts as a deterrent to many Jews. They have their own peculiar faults of character—selfishness, love of money and material prosperity, habits of lying, doubtful commercial dealings, lack of the sense of sin, in some countries, drunkenness and impurity. The stricter challenge of Christian morality causes a revolution in his moral outlook and in many cases the change seems too radical.

(*b*) *Intellectual Hindrances.*—The one-sided intellectual training of the Jew constitutes an obstacle to a full appreciation of the intellectual resources of Christianity. His acquired or inherited prejudice keeps him from giving fair and impartial consideration. His pride and self-sufficiency make him regard Christianity as something inferior to his own traditional faith. When he does give thought to the religion he is invited to accept as something better than his own, two considerations give him pause: (1) The inconsistency and indifference of the great mass of professed Christians whom he knows—"90 per cent of those who call themselves Christians," says one of them, "do not follow Christ;" and (2) the unceasing disruption of Christianity into denominations and sects. This, he argues, shows that Christianity is not sure of itself, and it makes it difficult for him to decide which Church or sect comes nearest to the truth of things.

(*c*) *Social Hindrances.*—These include the fear of consequences involved in any changing of his faith. Jews are peculiarly dependent on each other, and to break away means social and economic boycott. He would be left without the means of livelihood and in some districts exposed to persecution. His treatment by non-Jews does not dispose him favourably to seek their society and contempt, for the proselyte both from the side of the Jew and the Christian is a factor which he has to recognise. Anti-Semitism and the memory of Christian persecutions are also powerful factors. His strong racial feeling makes him regard his loss of membership of the Jewish race as a real sacrifice. The much canvassed tenets of Bolshevism with its indifference to or hostility against religion act also as a positive hindrance.

(*d*) *Political Hindrances.*—These are reported as disappearing. In Palestine reference is made to the law with regard to change of faith, but for most other countries political hindrances are declared negligible.

Many of these hindrances rest on wrong Jewish conceptions and sometimes on the unhistorical presentation of the Christian Message and will be overcome in time.

Anti-Semitism in many parts is decreasing and the social boycott of the Jew declining, but most correspondents report no great change with regard to these hindrances, while some bear witness to a stiffening of opposition to Christianity.

The majority of the writers have been content to enumerate the types of Jews found in the country they are dealing with and have ignored the question regarding the different missionary methods employed with respect to the different types. From the answers received, it is evident that the missionary method must vary according to the individual rather than the type. Each type of Jew does not yield to a uniform treatment. The Sephardim are easier to reach than the Ashkenazim—the Reform than the Orthodox, but special circumstances must be taken into consideration, one writer stating that the unemployed are easiest to reach.

While the question of Jewish Nationalism in relation to the Christian Message does not seem to be acute in many fields, in others the Jewish National movement shows itself distinctly hostile to Christianity through fear of breaking down national solidarity. This can be met by the Christian worker pointing out that acceptance of Christianity does not mean loss of nationality. "The Christian Message," one writer states, "must emphasise the greater value of our heavenly citizenship," and another "Christianity takes no account of nationality." Here, it is manifest, the line must be drawn strictly between political and religious considerations and pronouncement made that uniformity of religious belief does not necessarily mean uniformity of political opinion. "Zionism," says one writer, "which is so favourably disposed to the personality of Jesus as a man and a Jew, is just as fanatically hostile to Christianity."

Most of the correspondents make no discrimination in the attitude of Orthodox and Reform Judaism towards the Christian Message. "The usual antagonism," says one; "both very hostile," says another. Holland finds the Orthodox more accessible than the Reformed, while Germany has it that Orthodoxy is more positively hostile, and the Liberals are more apologetic before the comparison of Judaism and Christianity. The distinction is drawn by one writer: "Orthodox Judaism is a system of works and bargaining; Christianity a reception of grace and thanksgiving. Reformed Judaism is an attempt to solve the problem of the filching of Christian morality and teaching without the essentials"—"a half-way house to Christianity that most often becomes a terminus."

Summing up the above results of the Questionnaire, the conviction is strengthened that the presentation of the Christian Message to the Jew is a personal thing—it is the contact of life with life that counts. No one method is adequate for Jewry as a whole. It is the Gospel for the individual that is needed, so we are not surprised that the aspects of the Christian Message which have been found most effective in the practical experience of workers are many and varied. All are agreed upon the necessity of a friendly spirit and a personal testimony "to show the Jews the example of a true Christian life." The Jew is critical of a Christianity that does not live up to its profession, and the value of sincerity and purity of motive cannot be estimated too highly. Different writers place a different emphasis on the contents of the Message to be delivered, most laying stress on the need of redemption and the offer of forgiveness through Christ. The Love of God revealed in Christ, Christ and Him Crucified, the Gospel of the Crucified and Risen Lord, Christ as the Light of the World, the Kingdom of God, the effect of Christ's Teaching and Life on the World, Christ's Way of Life and Estimate of the infinite value of every individual are predominant in the minds of some workers, while others prefer to bring forward the priceless heritage common to Jew and Christian—"The Old and New Testaments in popular and evangelical form," "The New Testament as the fulfilment of much that is taught in the Old Testament," "The predictions of Scripture regarding the Messiah and the Jews," "The method of the Epistle to the Hebrews." One gives "a simple and straightforward exposition of the Gospels," while another presents "a Jewish Christ, one of their own race whose teaching is the religion of the prophets."

From the experience of many minds, may the great truths of the Christian Message become clearer to our souls and find adequate expression in the hearts and lives of our workers for the ingathering of Israel.

IV. EVANGELISATION

The missionary impulse and motive must be wholly spiritual, springing from obedience to Christ and Christian love to those who know not His salvation, but they must find expression in suitable and effective means of approach, of sympathetic conveyance of the contents of the Christian Message and of commending it by the influence of a gracious Christ-filled personality.

Missions mean methods—scientific, business-like methods, and the more methodical and efficient a mission is the more chance has it of being successful and its results permanent. The proclamation of the Gospel that is not followed up by teaching, by the care and spiritual development of the convert in a Christian atmosphere, is likely to be spasmodic and its gains squandered. The value of the Questionnaire will be judged for the most part by its ability to provide Jewish Mission agencies with a clear view of the best and most effective means of evangelisation, with a survey of their relative success in different circumstances, and with an authoritative indication of the best common policy to be pursued in the future. In this section the experience of those most closely in touch with Jewish missionary effort is summed up, and from it and from the discussions at the Conferences much mutual benefit can confidently be anticipated.

As is to be expected, many methods have been employed and most of them can claim successful results at one point or other. It is evident from the answers received, that there must be a considerable degree of elasticity and power of adaptation in the methods employed. Machinery that works well in one country may not produce the same results in another. The methods above everything must be made suitable for the persons to be reached. There is no one stereotyped method applicable to all circumstances. The common element in all successful forms of missionary activity is personal dealing—the primary method of missions in the Gospel—the heart to heart talk whether in school, or mission-house or hospital—the personal testimony as to what the Lord hath done for us. This can never be a mechanical matter—the less machinery here the better—method must vary with every inquiring individual, but the power of a consecrated personality is essential.

the demand is made (from Poland) that "the Jew must be converted and believe in Jesus Christ as Son of God and Messiah. Each Jew before Baptism is instructed in the promises of God regarding the Messiah and in the ethics of apostolic teaching."

Government Regulations regarding (*a*) the age at which candidates for Baptism may be received into the Christian Church and (*b*) open-air preaching have been reported as follows :—

Austria : (*a*) 14 years. Permission required for (*a*) and (*b*).

Czecho-Slovakia: (*a*) No law for persons over 16. Parents or guardians decide for those under 16. (*b*) Open-air meetings must be announced beforehand to magistrates, but, generally speaking, no difficulty made *now*.

Denmark : (*a*) No law for persons of 18 : permission of parents necessary up to 18.

Finland : (*a*) 18 years ; (*b*) Police permission necessary.

Germany : (*a*) None ; (*b*) Permissible, but small police fee necessary.

Greece : (*a*) Must be of age ; (*b*) Not permitted.

Hungary : (*a*) 18 years ; (*b*) Police permission necessary.

Poland : (*a*) None ; (*b*) Agencies which have Government sanction get police permission.

Rumania : (*a*) 21 ; proposed new law 18 ; (*b*) Not permitted.

Transylvania : (*a*) Special laws—Bill of Cults ; (*b*) special permission required, generally forbidden.

Egypt : (*a*) Not known ; (*b*) Not permitted, but terms of law unknown.

Palestine : (*a*) No regulation for Baptism, but official recognition of religious status necessary after change of religion—age 20 ; (*b*) Turkish law prohibiting, but terms unknown ; considered inadvisable if not illegal.

Tunisia : (*a*) None ; (*b*) strictly prohibited.

Turkey : (*a*) None ; (*b*) General law against all forms of religious propaganda. Police permission necessary for every type of meeting.

The reports from different countries indicate that the problem of finding means of livelihood for converted Jews is real and pressing. In many cases conversion means loss of employment, especially if, as so often happens, the convert's employer is a Jew. The missionary necessarily feels some responsibility in the matter, and various methods are attempted to secure employment. The warning is given that no promise of employment should be made before conversion or Baptism, and in some Societies the practice is to baptise only those who have assured means of existence. There is unanimity that material assistance should only be given in exceptional circumstances and one Society has absolutely abolished such help. The abuse of indiscriminate charity can best be guarded against by finding employment for the convert, by an understanding amongst Societies to avoid indiscriminate relief, and by "each convert receiving a certificate of character from missionary who has been the means of converting him." To meet this problem many are in favour of establishing industrial institutions, teaching trades to converts, *e.g.* basket-making, gardening; Persia suggests carpentry, market-gardening, glass-making for men, and cotton-cleaning, carpet-weaving and embroidery for women. Agricultural colonies are recommended by some, but owing to the fewness of converts at many stations it is felt that this work could best be done by some central authority, and the Hebrew Christian Alliance is suggested by one writer. Others with some experience in the matter are opposed to special industrial work for Jewish converts and consider it best to bring converts into touch with Christian merchants and manufacturers with a view to obtaining employment. "Nothing should be done to make converts a class by themselves, separate from Jews and Christians. The convert should rank as a Christian pure and simple and be employed by Christian employers as such."

While some missions adopt no special means for maintaining and developing the spiritual life of converts, others pay particular attention to this matter. They are "received into the community of believers in the Church and contact with other Hebrew Christians," and most Societies encourage their converts to join a church and undertake responsibility for definite Christian service. They are regularly visited and personal relations maintained, help being given them to find Christian friends and connections. Special meetings are arranged—Sunday services and Bible classes, and in several places there are unions of Jewish Christians and branches of the International Hebrew Christian Alliance.

The Jew on conversion is expected to take part in missionary work by the testimony of his life and his zeal in Christian service. They are "specially valuable when used as voluntary workers," "the Jews being suspicious of Hebrew Christians employed as paid workers." Those who have outstanding gifts for missionary work can be employed as paid agents, "only with great caution," writes one, "after long training" and "under supervision of non-Jewish missionary," write others. The lack of special institutions for training them is deplored, and advantage is taken in many cases of Christian Bible schools. Warsaw "hopes to have Training Home by time of Conferences."

A very decided cleavage of opinion is apparent in the views that have been ascertained regarding the employment of Jewish *versus* Gentile Christians in Jewish mission work. The contrast can be marked in the following sentences: "Jewish Christians more suitable." "It is a mistake to send out Hebrew missionaries. Non-Jewish missionaries have advantage of more spiritually developed characters, and do not raise such prejudices as Jews." "In some cases Hebrew Christian missionaries are very effective and desirable." "Very few Hebrew Christian missionaries are fit for leadership." "Hope for evangelisation of the Jews lies in Hebrew Christians." "Well-trained Gentile Christians are the better missionaries to the Jews." The balance of opinion is in favour of the Gentile missionary.

Many of the writers have avoided the comparison of the relative merits of Jew and non-Jew missionary and have seen the ideal system in co-operation between the two. "A combination seems desirable, 80 per cent Jewish Christians and 20 per cent Gentile." "Both, if consecrated, are useful. The Jewish Christian has superior knowledge of his people and their teaching, but the Gentile Christian is not regarded as a turn-coat and renegade." "Jewish Christians are better for colportage and itineracy; for station work a Gentile as head with Hebrew Christian colleagues." "Gentile and Hebrew Christians should work together, the one giving the initiative, the other supplying 'local colour.'"

Most of the correspondents have simply stated the number of converts at their own stations since 1900, and no figures are available for estimating the converts in the whole area or in neighbouring countries. It may be taken that the figures given refer only to converts to Protestantism. Many Societies keep no definite records, so the returns are necessarily incomplete. Twenty-four missionaries in Europe have given figures, and these bring the number of their converts since 1900 up to 2184. In the Presbyterian Church of America there have been between 1000 and 2000 converts, 55 of whom are ordained missionaries. In the United States it is estimated there have been about 20,000 converts, of whom about 1000 are Roman Catholics.

These converts are generally received sympathetically into the native Christian Churches, only in very few cases is complaint made of unsympathetic treatment. "The Churches do little for them," says one writer. Where there exists suspicion of them, time, education and Christian sympathy should bring a remedy. Very few Hebrew Christian congregations have been formed, in most places the number of converts being too small. "Efforts to found Hebrew Christian congregations have been going on in Germany. The International Conference in Stockholm in 1911 took this up without result." In Poland converts are "sometimes formed into Hebrew Christian congregations, some treated in a friendly fashion but generally with suspicion." "One case of a Hebrew Christian congregation in Canada was discontinued on the advice of the Committee." Conflicting views are expressed on the question of a Hebrew Christian Church. Many feel it is a matter for the Hebrew Christians themselves to settle. Others hold very decided opinions on the question. "Hebrew Christians should attach themselves to the Church in which they were brought up, joining together as a people, knowing they have a message for their race. Hebrew Christian communities can be formed only out of an evangelical movement (as in Russia)." "Not in favour of a Hebrew Christian Church," "not desirable," "not practicable," "tending to division of the Body of Christ" are some of the opinions expressed.

"A Hebrew Christian Church is hopeless, but Hebrew Christian Union (interconfessional) necessary." "A Hebrew Christian Church is impossible until a strong one is formed in Palestine and there is a Jewish state. At present Hebrew Christian associations should be formed."

Many, on the other hand, are in favour of such a Church, considering it would prove a real service, and others regard it as an ideal to be realised in the future.

Evidence is adduced as to the prevalence of emigration amongst converts, from 8 per cent in one district to

80 per cent in another leaving the country of their conversion, but on the whole the tendency and opportunities to emigrate are decreasing.

It is surprising to find that many Societies keep no register of converts. Those connected with Churches keep a Baptismal register and the certificate of Baptism serves as a certificate of Church membership. There is little or no co-operation between the several missions with regard to converts. Occasional correspondence on particular cases seems to be the only means and the need of urgent improvement is indicated. Converts from one mission are generally welcomed by other missions, unless when these missions are connected with Churches. In this case the rules and regulations of the Church concerned are imposed on the convert desiring to join. "Denominationalism," says one writer, "is the difficulty. The convert must join a particular Church. Sometimes he is re-baptised before admittance. There should be no emphasis laid on points of difference in doctrine. It creates difficulties."

V. CHRISTIAN EDUCATION

The teaching function of the Church has been recognised in all the Christian centuries. Christ not only preached the Gospel, but He taught His disciples and the people. His lessons on the way of life are an education in themselves, and the spirit of His teaching has inspired a mighty host of those who sought to bring light and learning to the minds of men. His Great Commission enjoins teaching as one of its imperatives, and in the forefront of educational progress His Church has always moved till the day came when the greater part of its teaching ministry was taken out of its hands by the State or by modern educational institutions.

Missionary societies have followed the same line of progress. In many countries the mission school has been and is the one centre of light and knowledge. The modern demand of education for all has forced schools to arise in nearly every town and village, but the mission agencies still find scope for valuable educational service. On all hands appreciation is expressed of the splendid work done in mission schools often with very meagre resources and equipment, and the names of missionary teachers are held in high honour in many lands.

In Jewish missions education has played an important part, and abundant testimony is borne by those who answered the Questionnaire to its value and helpfulness. "Most useful branch of mission work for Jews," says one, and "education is one of the Church's greatest opportunities. Jews are extremely keen on an English education," says another, writing from Egypt. "Christian education breaks down barriers and prejudice. The general influence is good, but stops too early—needs following up." "School work in the past," testifies another, "has been of great service. When real Christian atmosphere is in the school, the influence is felt in later life, although no definite profession of faith in Christ is made." Few of the correspondents have faced the question of the relative usefulness of the different grades of school, and some of those who answered have missed the point of the question. There is only one categorical statement: "Influence felt most in elementary schools."

The supervision of education by the State is undertaken in several countries where there is no State provision of schools. The Educational Code lays down the Government requirements, and sometimes these bear hardly on mission establishments. In Rumania the Government recognises private schools. In the first four classes the State programme must be taken; in further classes a special programme may be adopted, provided Rumanian is taken. By special permission, Saturday and Sunday are free, and certain subjects can be taught in German. A new law has been passed which if applied will make all school work impossible. In Hungary the Scottish Mission has freedom, but no Government grants are accepted. Transylvania reports, "In addition to State schools, all the different religious bodies have their own schools recognised by the State (*e.g.* Reformed, Lutheran, Roman Catholic, Unitarian, Jewish, etc.). There are private schools. By the latest Education Act, December 1925, schools cannot be founded by educational societies, spiritual orders or school congregations which are dependent on another State. Foreign subjects cannot be principals of schools."

The Education Code in Turkey has only been in force for one year—the only part as yet enforced is that concerning the compulsory teaching of Turkish in all schools.

The attitudes of Governments to mission schools vary—some are friendly, others are distinctly hostile. In Germany it is reported, "Missions schools impossible—they would serve no purpose as Christian religion would be excluded." This is the same attitude as is found in Holland, in Rumania, where the new law forbids all propaganda among children and parents, and in Transylvania. In other countries there is no Government opposition, but the ample provision of educational facilities makes mission schools more or less unnecessary.

The aims of missionary education are generally agreed upon as a good general education, Bible-teaching, instruction in and development of Christian character, winning for Christ. The mission school is an excellent means of removing deep-rooted prejudice and establishing a better understanding between Jew and Christian.

Apart from new or better premises and some local requirements the greatest needs indicated are for trained teachers, kindergartens, and in one case a science laboratory.

Any weaknesses of educational missions have not been pointed out, though one writer draws attention to the danger of the appointment of teachers without the missionary spirit, of routine and soul-less teaching of the Bible, of undue or one-sided stress on educational work. "If the educational side is co-ordinated with evangelistic, and if the educational staff has true missionary spirit, there are few better missionary instruments."

The place of Bible teaching in mission schools is paramount—nothing can take its place and no matter what goes Bible teaching must be maintained. Our Christian education is based on its teaching and its spirit. It produces results—nothing else produces results like it, and in all Jewish Mission work it holds and must hold first place. It is the great power to give new life, to reveal the way of life, to break down prejudice, to create and sustain moral character. If the children of our mission schools are children of the Book, our labour is not in vain in the Lord. Pupils who have been taught the Bible at school show the effects in their characters. They often reveal a knowledge and understanding of the New Testament which is surprising, and many of them become Christian at heart, and from them many baptisms result. Several writers have pointed out the results manifest particularly in the second generation of pupils taught in mission schools. Children of old scholars have a Christian background to life and no prejudices to break down. So valuable does the teaching of the Book seem that the majority state that attendance at Bible lesson on the part of the scholars should be compulsory—not in any harsh way, but it should be taken for granted and " all pupils come "—" no one has ever complained." While compulsory attendance at Bible teaching is preferable, it is conceded that attendance at religious services should be voluntary. One writer advocates voluntary attendance at Bible lessons as well—" otherwise some may think Christianity or Christian teaching is the penalty involved in obtaining the good education which these schools undoubtedly give." " Compulsory in lower classes, voluntary in upper classes " is the practice urged by one writer. If the Bible is prohibited and direct missionary appeal forbidden, is the Christian atmosphere of the school sufficient for missionary purposes ? There is unanimity that it is not. " Teachers must be living Christians and show that the Christian belief is penetrating. They ought to aim at definite conversions." " At all costs," urges one, " the Bible lesson must be held on to." A mission school without the Bible is like a gun without ammunition, or, if that illustration is too militaristic, like a receiving set without aerial attachment.

While education in some mission schools is free, in the great majority fees are paid with special consideration shown to poor people and many free places for those who can pay nothing. " Parents are willing to pay fees in Higher Schools according to their means, especially Jewish parents who sacrifice much for the education of their children." " What is not paid for is not appreciated." If fees are not charged the schools are laid open to the charge of special inducements. The practice, however, in some schools is to provide free education, but if fees are offered willingly they are accepted.

The question of the proportion of income received from fees to the total cost of the educational work has been answered only by three writers, and it is indicated as 75 per cent, 60 per cent, and 20 per cent.

The bulk of opinion is in favour of Christian Homes for Jewish children. " If possible, would be invaluable to get children out of their environment. In reality, however, it is not generally possible, as poorest Jewish parents would rather let their children die of hunger than be defiled by non-kosher food." "Found invaluable," is the verdict from Jerusalem.

There seems to be no practical difficulty in correlating educational work and evangelism. The educational work of mission schools is generally based on the Gospel—the teachers are Christian missionaries and the atmosphere is that of Christian sympathy and love. Through the scholars contact is readily made with Jewish homes and a Christian influence brought to bear on the parents and other members of the family. Visitors should be attached to every school. The older pupils and old scholars usually attract outsiders to special meetings.

A Central Jewish Missionary Education Committee would be desirable, but it is Utopian! "Centralisation is always desirable and should be vested in an undenominational body such as the International Hebrew Christian Alliance, which would be able to deal with the educational situation for students of all countries, where a Hebrew Christian environment could be created and special attention paid to suitable Hebrew Christians who desire to be trained for the ministry or the mission field."

No further suggestions on Christian education of any practical value have been elicited.

VI. MEDICAL MISSIONS

The reports may fall into two groups, those from countries highly civilised and those from "backward" countries.

In the former, the reports give the impression that there is no absolute need for Medical Missions. These countries have an efficient medical service and an unlimited number of doctors, and it is not necessary for Christian Societies to take up this form of work. Turkey demands Turkish Diplomas, so that medical work there is impossible under Christian auspices, unless a European has a Turkish Diploma, or a Turkish subject is Protestant, and interested in Christian Missions. Rumania also demands a Rumanian qualification, and a foreigner would find this difficult to get for various reasons. In France, there is no medical work done among the Jews. In Germany, it is not favoured, according to the report, which states that religious services are held in public infirmaries, where any Jews present do not object. In Holland, there is no medical work; and the same information comes from Sweden. Norway has a medical work with two nurses at Galatz, Rumania. U.S.A. and South Africa have no medical work. In Canada, the medical work was discontinued, as there was very little need for it, and those who came for assistance gave the impression they came because they got it for nothing.

There is no medical work in Egypt, and as far as Alexandria is concerned, it is not necessary. In Transylvania, there is no occasion for such work, as there is a plentiful supply of doctors (some of whom are Jewish) and well-equipped State hospitals So in Hungary also.

The second group indicates clearly that where the country is backward, and frequently the Jews are gathered in poor quarters, there is a definite need for medical work. At one centre in Greece there is a daily dispensary, and it is described as needful and effective. Tunis is overfull of doctors. In Abyssinia, medical work is most necessary, although there is none at present. On a journey through Abyssinia of over 1000 miles, only two doctors were met with, and they were connected with a Consulate. One report states that for hygienic reasons, medical work is necessary, for the Jews of that area are dirty and unhealthy.

Midway between these two groups, there are countries like Palestine and Syria, where medical work is a valuable adjunct to any work that may be carried on by the authorities—in these two countries, by the British and French respectively.

Not one report deals with the question of definite results, but wherever this form of work is employed, it is appreciated by the Jews who support it. There is a suggestion in one report that this work raises the opposition of Jews who do not support it.

There are no proposals put forward for securing a greater degree of efficiency, or for the correlation and development of medical work in stationary spheres with itineracy.

The Questionnaire asks whether compulsory or voluntary attendance at religious services is preferable. The answers state that in the greater number of cases attendance is voluntary, a practice which the majority would favour. In only one or two cases is compulsory attendance preferred.

Fees are not generally charged for medical advice, unless it is clear that the patient can afford these. Generally, the medicine is charged for, but the amount from this source is trifling. In Greece, free medicine is given to the poorest.

The question regarding maternity hospitals is not directly answered, but a number express the view that private or district nursing would be acceptable.

There are no suggestions regarding the correlation of medical and evangelistic work, except through preaching. From Germany comes the view that the use of medical work for the propagation of evangelistic preaching has the effect of being interpreted as proselytism.

Regarding indigenous agents or institutions, the answers vary. In Greece, such agents "cannot be usefully employed." Rumania is not ready for indigenous assistance. There is apparently no objection to the services of indigenous agents in Palestine, except that they are rarely interested in the presentation of Christianity to the Jew.

Summary

Anti-Semitic feeling does not appear to exist anywhere in hospitals, and Jews are admitted irrespective of nationality. Jews show no antipathy to Christian doctors or nurses, or to religious services in hospitals.

The great amount of medical activity appears to be among women and children. Although it is not suggested by the reports, a possible reason for this may be that, owing to the status of Jewish women, they have learned that they receive more sympathetic treatment in a Christian institution.

The principle of medical work among Jews can be supported on the ground that in some parts of the East the Jews are utterly neglected, and live in insanitary conditions, so that as a piece of Christian community service this should be done. In cases of civilised countries, where the need for medical work scarcely arises, it should be governed by considerations of absolute need, and not carried on in rivalry with medical work supported by Jews, without the suggestion that cheap medicine or any other accompaniment has the implication in it of a bribe.

One striking case is reported in connection with a dispensary, where a woman was attending out of friendliness to the Christian institution, because, when living in Europe, and having the experience of a pogrom, she received medical treatment at Christian hands, her husband having been killed.

VII. CHRISTIAN LITERATURE

In the review of *The Present Situation in Jewry*, it is stated that, on the religious side, it was reported from country after country that the majority of educated Jews had turned to agnosticism or atheism; that religious apathy and indifference were growing apace; that Orthodoxy was being rapidly undermined; and that, with no small proportion of Jews, Zionism and Nationalism were taking the place of religious faith. From the point of view of the missionary, this means that he is confronted to-day with problems his predecessors had but little to deal with—problems that must be met by methods and with weapons essentially differing from theirs.

It is, therefore, not to be wondered at that, with few exceptions, missionaries everywhere complain of the inadequacy, or unsuitability, of the missionary literature at their disposal. Some go so far as to describe almost all the available books and tracts as antiquated and out of date; while others (and perhaps with better judgment) suggest a thorough revision of the existing literature along with the provision of new publications, calculated to meet the requirements of the new conditions and the changed outlook on life.

The breaking up of the Ghettoes in Eastern Europe, with the consequent spread of Western ideas and education among the Jews there, is also affecting the linguistic problem. While formerly publications in Yiddish and Hebrew were practically all that was wanted in a large section of the mission field, it is found now that many Jews are no more acquainted, or not sufficiently familiar, with these idioms, and generally prefer literature printed in the language of their native country, be this English, German or French, Dutch, Russian or Polish, Hungarian, Rumanian or Arabic. Palestine clamours for more and more Hebrew.

Since illiteracy is practically unknown among Jews (as

far, at least, as the men are concerned), the value of good literature, as an aid to mission work, can hardly be overestimated. It is claimed for it from many a quarter, that it will often go where the missionary cannot; that it will penetrate doors closed to him; that it will bring home to an inquirer truths that could only briefly be touched on in conversation; and that many a conversion, or the inpulse to it, can be traced back to the reading of a tract that had accidentally fallen into the hands of a Jew.

So far the consensus of opinion is pretty unanimous; but not so with regard to the best method of circulation of literature. Some would have the New Testament and tracts given away free of charge, and scattered with a liberal hand. Others contend that, where people can afford it, they should be made to pay, since things obtained for nothing are apt to be slighted and little thought of. And yet others think that portions of Scripture and tracts should only be offered after preceding conversation, or at the close of a meeting, when a certain amount of interest has been created, and the subject discussed can thus be further driven home. Promiscuous distribution they entirely condemn. On the other hand, the colporteurs of the London Society in Rumania and of the Scottish Mission in Hungary have for many years been able to sell large numbers of missionary tracts and Bibles, and they are generally received with a certain friendliness.

From this it is evident that no fast and dry rules can be laid down on the subject, and that local conditions and peculiarities must necessarily be taken into consideration, but whenever a request for literature comes from Jews themselves, they should be made to pay for it, if at all able to do so.

As to the men one could hope to see turning out the much needed tracts, it is worth noting, as illustrating the peculiar difficulty of the subject, that not only have no offers been received from any quarter to contribute suitable treatises, but that no names of persons capable and willing to do so, and who might be approached on the matter, have even been suggested by any of our numerous correspondents. Some advise the committees of the various missionary societies to set aside suitable people to prepare new tracts; others would like to see a list of subjects drawn up, substantial prizes offered, and writers invited to compete for them; while others again pertinently remark that the writing of good tracts cannot be done to order, but that men of vision, men who have a message to deliver, should be encouraged to do so in their own way, and send their contributions to a central office.

No less divided are the opinions on the question whether converts, Gentile missionaries, or theologians generally are to be entrusted with the work. Gentiles are inclined to question the amount of spiritual experience, and even the mental equipment, converts can bring to this task, while some of the latter, in their turn, are sceptical about the correct knowledge of matters Jewish, and the sympathetic appreciation of the difficulties of a Jew, possessed by the average Gentile. It is also apprehended that the learned theologian is apt to be dry, if not pedantic, while good writing, with a dash of "journalism," is of the essence of a really good tract.

On one thing only all are here agreed, and that is the desirability of co-operation in the production of literature. At present, however, it is only the German societies that have achieved this object at home and are in the habit of interchanging their missionary publications. The London Society did the same for some time in Great Britain, but did not meet with any reciprocity.

There remains but to say a word about literature for the home base, and for Christians generally, on the subject of Jewish missions. This would seem to be in a much more satisfactory condition than that intended for Jews. Some of the writings of Adolph Saphir, David Baron, John Wilkinson, Sidney, Bernstein, and others, in English, as well as those of Gurland, de le Roi, etc., in German, continue to answer their purpose. Missionary magazines should be made as readable, bright, and interesting as possible. Biographies of Jewish Christians of note are always well received. The duty of evangelising the Jews should be impressed upon the consciousness of the Church.

No special literature for converts is needed where good Christian literature is otherwise available.

VIII. OCCUPATION OF THE FIELD

The reports are fragmentary, and the impression left by them is that of disappointment—a vast, unoccupied field, and where occupied by Christian Churches or by Missions to the people of the countries, little or nothing done for the Jew. This is the substance of the reports, not only from Greece, Gibraltar, India, Trinidad, Africa, Australia, New Zealand, Japan, but from France, Italy, Portugal, Czecho-Slovakia, Denmark and other countries.

Turkey ignores Foreign Missions almost entirely, and with the exception of the Scottish Mission and the Mission of the American Board (in which there is a slight degree of interest), nothing is done for the Jew. In Austria, work has only begun, and therefore there is no point of view as yet. Belgium expresses the hope that before long the Protestant Churches will do something. In Czecho-Slovakia, where there is little interest in Foreign Missions, but which interest is developing, the need is for more information on the subject of the Jews. In Tunisia, the French tendency to Anti-Semitism affects the local attitude to Jewish Missions ; there are no native Christian Churches in this area at present.

The language of the Jew is generally that of the country in which he lives with the addition of one or two other languages, Yiddish being the most general. In Finland, the Jews speak Yiddish, Finish, Swedish ; in Poland, Polish, Yiddish, and Russian ; in Transylvania, Yiddish, Hungarian, and (since the accession of Transylvania to Rumania) many Jews are conversant with Rumanian.

Sweden reports that many of the Jews belong to old Swedish-Jewish families, often well-educated. As in the case of Germany, only those Jews in Sweden who are immigrants from Eastern Europe speak Yiddish. The situation in Sweden is such that the reports consider no more workers are necessary in Sweden. In Norway, the Jews are mostly of lower classes, German or Polish. The Christian efforts there do not touch the higher-class Jew.

In Holland, the Jews have become merged, and have lost their own language and do not understand Yiddish. Only few know Hebrew. The intellectual class is not touched, and there is a great need for colportage work in this country. Another report from Holland states that hardly any illiterate Jews are found. Some of the Jews speak German, in addition to Dutch.

Poland reports that about one-third of the Jews are Orthodox. All are more or less educated. Nearly half belong to the better class, being in professions (doctors, lawyers) and business. A great many of the Orthodox

Jews are small shopkeepers and "middlemen." The degree of Communism is negligible. These remarks apply mainly to Warsaw. In other parts of Poland, the Jews are mostly poor, although in White Russia (where at present the poverty among the peasants is great) the Jew is relatively rich, being the trader and shopkeeper of this part. In the eastern parts of Poland, Polish is spoken by the Jews. An interesting fact is recorded from Poland that the rich Jew is sometimes found without education, and the poor Jew is sometimes intellectual. In the small towns of Poland 80 per cent of the Jews are not reached by Christian Missions. Altogether, Poland appears to be a great field for evangelistic activity.

Hungary reports that, in a city like Budapest, the Jews belong to various strata, mainly middle-class. In intellectual attainment the standard is of the highest. In religion they are Orthodox and Neologue, but in religious attitude they are nominally Orthodox. A large mass of intellectual Jews (mainly materialistic) is untouched.

In Rumania, similar reports are to hand of the need and the sphere. The Jews of Rumania are estimated at 950,000, and spheres like Galatz and Jassy are mentioned. Colporteurs are needed for Bessarabia. The majority of Rumanian Jews are Orthodox, but ignorant of things spiritual. Languages used are Rumanian, Yiddish, Russian. The Bucarest Jew speaks German, the Transylvanian Jew Hungarian, the Old Kingdom Jew Rumanian. Centres like Cernovitz need to be occupied. It is estimated that in Transylvania alone there are 300,000 Jews, and only one missionary is there, he having begun work a year ago. This area is practically untouched. The Jews are Orthodox, "Reformed" and indifferent. The classes are very rich and very poor—merchants, operatives, street-vendors, etc. The standard of education is from general to highest degree. The Transylvanian Jews know German.

There are several reports from Germany. The Jews there are of all classes, but the "Intellectuals" are barely touched. There is room for all methods and forces, and colportage work in small towns is useful. The relations between the Jews and Christian Churches are friendly. Another report states that the greater number of German Jews assimilate to the "Reform" Jews, but the range is from moderate Orthodoxy (more or less "progressive") to Pantheism, resulting in a religion of philosophical, ethical Agnosticism. Germany emphasises the need of workers; and stress is laid on this report (and in others) of the necessity of having highly trained and educated workers among Jews. One report states "the qualifications of workers are not in relation to the intellectual Jewish standpoint." Holland suggests that the powers of laymen and women might be better developed for work among the Jews. Turkey asks for literature of a high standard, dealing with Christianity from an "apologetic" point of view. In Germany, the greater number of Jews are well-to-do, and belong to the educated class. They speak German, and only those who come from Eastern Europe speak Yiddish. A certain "aristocracy" exists among them, and in some parts—especially in West and South—a small Jewish citizenship is recognised. These creditable and solid elements are, however, disappearing among the Jews of large towns.

Contrasted with the conditions outside Europe, those in other countries vary greatly. In Tunisia every trade and profession is carried on by the Jew. There is little class-distinction. The older type of native Jew is perhaps two-thirds of the whole. The other third is the Italian Jew, living almost as the Europeans. The younger type of native Jew is in the transition stage. All speak Arabic, some French and Italian. Only in the capital of Tunisia is there Christian work among Jews. There are a few independent workers in Morocco who do not co-operate or co-ordinate.

In Persia, the status of the Jew is good; a request is made for two educated missionaries for Ispahan, and also for a welfare worker. An itinerary evangelist is also required for South Persia, where the Jews would help; and similar needs for North Persia. In Abyssinia, most "falashas" are artisans, clean and thrifty, but despised by other Abyssinians. The language is Am-haric. The central part of the country where these live is now opening out to European missionaries. There are about 80,000, very scattered. Many workers are required for this area. At Aden Settlement, there are no illiterate Jews, but the educational standard is mainly low. In Egypt, the Jews rank from the poorest to the richest, and in education and intelligence are distinctly in advance. The languages spoken are various tongues; but very little Hebrew is known. In Turkey, no data about areas and numbers are available. The present Christian activity is small, consisting mainly of work among poorer Jews and lower middle-class (family traders).

In Palestine, all classes of Jews are influenced, the Jews being divided by one report, as—commercial 60 per cent, Haluzim 25 per cent, religious and professional 15 per cent; and the social classification as—upper 10 per cent, middle 45 per cent, lower 45 per cent. Hebrew is generally spoken. The upper class is seldom touched, except occasionally in conversation. In social intercourse in Jerusalem, there is friendliness between Jew and Christian. This city is proportionately overmanned with workers, and there is a prospect of more, while the needs of the country are not sufficiently attended to, and redistribution is desirable.

These reports deal with the remaining items of this section of the Questionnaire, and briefly are:—

The unoccupied areas are numerous with vast populations that can only be estimated. No statistics are available. The German Societies have divided the areas of their own country among themselves, and are critical towards non-German Societies, specifying in one case a Society which should leave Germany and go to Poland and Galicia. The German statistics in Schneider's Year-Book are reliable; for the use of other Societies, these statistics could be obtained in the form of reprints from the Year-Book.

One report thinks the Evangelistic opportunity is found among the Jews of Eastern Europe, who are immigrants of the various more civilised countries. The Swedish Society finds its activity in Vienna rather than in its own country. In the main, no overlapping among the Societies is reported. More co-operation is welcomed, except that the reports from Holland, Hungary, Palestine and Poland indicate that co-operation is not always practicable. One report from Germany favours co-operation between Societies "with great respect for boundaries." A report from Rumania states that co-operation must be cautious; "cannot seek co-operation with those who do not hold the Divinity of our Lord."

The attitude of Christian Churches is variously described; the native Protestant Churches of Switzerland are generally indifferent. The missionaries of the Friends of Israel, in Basel, are members of the Protestant Church, Poland. In Greece, the attitude of the Protestant Church is friendly.

In Holland, the Protestant Churches are not unfriendly, but are not sufficiently interested. In Hungary, the Protestant Churches on the whole are sympathetic, especially towards the Scottish Mission, Budapest. In Transylvania, the Church attitude is "just leave them alone." In Poland, the Lutheran is the only Church working under the Basel Mission (in Lodz), and often there is no contact with other Churches, although their pastors are sympathetic towards itinerant missionaries. In India, the Churches never (or seldom) mention Jewish Missions. In Germany, Churches ordain missionaries to the Jews, but are not financially responsible. In German Churches, in the General Common Prayer, on Sundays, Jewish Missions are remembered. Anti-Semitism is not reported among the Churches to a marked extent, but the Lutheran Church is affected by this movement; and another report from Germany, while stating that the Churches are not anti-Semitic, adds this statement, "that does not exclude the warding off of Jewish, anti-Christian encroachments."

The reports from Great Britain, America and Canada do not furnish details of work among Jews, but work in these countries is a very small portion of the activity of the Churches, being usually supported by interested persons. There is not much Anti-Semitism among the Churches of these countries, but a considerable amount of prejudice. A certain amount of co-operation exists, especially in Great Britain, and this would be greatly facilitated by the formation of a Board of representatives from the Societies working among English-speaking Jews.

IX. TRAINING AND EFFICIENCY OF MISSIONARIES

On hardly another subject would there seem to be such a preponderating amount of agreement in the mission field as on that of the training and efficiency of missionaries. All are agreed that Gentile as well as Jewish Christians are wanted; that missionaries cannot be too well educated; that knowledge of Hebrew is a *sine qua non*; and that the greatest care in the selection of would-be workers is imperative. All are equally agreed that, in addition to Hebrew, a missionary should strive to get a thorough command of the principal language of the country he is working in, as well as of the particular dialect spoken by the Jews; and that this can best be done in the country itself, if the missionary be allowed from one to two years for this special purpose, and is given every reasonable facility for study. In addition to this, a working knowledge of German (which most European Jews understand) and of Rabbinics will often be found very useful.

As to the enlistment and training of converts for mission work, heads of missions are advised to keep an eye on really promising and intelligent young men in their respective districts, encourage them to help in the work, and eventually to offer themselves for missionary service. But every baptised Jew must not regard himself as a potential missionary from the mere fact of his being a convert. A reasonable length of time should be allowed for testing the sincerity of a convert's faith and the stability of his Christian character before he be recommended for training at a school or seminary.

The principal items of instruction should be Biblical and theological, and a thorough knowledge of the text of the Bible should be aimed at, for it is essential for a missionary to be able to quote the Scriptures fluently and correctly—the Old Testament preferably in Hebrew. In addition to the ordinary theological subjects, a course of Jewish history up to our own times, a certain amount of Rabbinics, and a careful study of the Jewish objections to Christianity and how to meet them, should form part of the curriculum.

This applies to Gentiles as well, who will, in addition, find it absolutely necessary to acquaint themselves with the Jewish Prayer Book and with Jewish habits, customs, and ceremonies. Occasional visits to a synagogue will be found useful.

On the completion of his studies, the candidate should be engaged by the respective Society provisionally for one or two years and sent to work under an experienced missionary, whose advice and guidance he is to enjoy, and whose reports and opinion will assist his committee in their decision as to the further engagement of the candidate. A year's experience of actual mission work will also be sufficient to show the young man whether this be his true vocation in life or not.

As for the training institutions themselves, it is thought

that the Institutum Delitzschianum at Leipzig, a similar seminary in London, and one in the United States will suffice for all practical purposes, to meet the need of the whole of the Jewish mission field. Gentile students might join either for the whole course of studies, or if graduates of theological colleges, for the special Jewish subjects.

As a means of conserving a missionary's energy and safeguarding his continued usefulness, it is variously urged

(1) That he be adequately remunerated, so that he need not look out for incidental emoluments to augment his scanty stipend, and so divert some of his time from his proper avocation;

(2) That he be not left to carry on his work single-handed, but that each station should be provided with, at least, two workers to help and encourage each other, and to enjoy the Christian fellowship of prayer and friendly intercourse;

(3) That the missionary be as little as possible burdened with administrative and secretarial work, which leaves him but little time for spiritual ministrations ; and

(4) That opportunity be given to the missionaries of a district, or province, to come together, at certain intervals, for informal conference, study of Biblical and cognate subjects, and for the deepening of their spiritual life. A quickened spirituality is the best cure of staleness and loss of vigour.

Missionaries home on furlough are advised to devote the first month to rest and recreation, of which they will certainly stand in need after five or six years' honest work. The remainder of their time should be divided between deputation work, necessary studies, and the attendance of a conference or two for the deepening of their Christian life. Some recommend also visits to other missions in order to study other people's methods, and to profit by them. But in no circumstances should a missionary's furlough be made a continuous round of deputation work. This is not furlough, but merely a change in the kind of work.

Before setting out for the mission field, workers will do well to equip themselves with all the knowledge and information outlined above, and women workers will often find a knowledge of first-aid and nursing of considerable assistance in their dealing with the poorer classes of Jews.

Whatever may be said of the usefulness of language schools elsewhere, Jews are too widely scattered, and they speak too many languages and dialects to make the acquisition of them at any given school practicable. The languages of Western Europe can readily be acquired in a variety of ways, while the other tongues are best learned in the countries where they are spoken.

Finally, the question whether missionaries should be appointed for long or short periods is answered variously. Some think that it would obviate the necessity of providing pensions for disabled and retiring missionaries if the engagement were to run for a limited number of years, and the missionary then went back to ordinary parochial work, or to any other occupation. But the great majority are in favour of appointment for long periods. "Jewish work," says an old missionary with experience of work in different countries, "needs a lifetime of experience. Short service men would hardly be fitted for work by the time they had to leave." "Short-timers," says another experienced missionary, "rarely take things seriously enough. It takes many years to form an efficient worker, not to speak of an expert at all."

X. SPIRITUAL POWER

Prayer and meditation, and the study of God's Word, are generally recognised to be the source of all spiritual power, and wherever a number of missionaries are stationed together, and especially where these are augmented by the teaching staff of a mission school, prayer-meetings and Bible readings are held regularly once a week. In places where there are also missionaries of other societies at work, as is the case in several Moslem countries, united meetings for prayer, and occasional conferences, are held as well, and are greatly appreciated as a means of spiritual uplifting. But all this is denied to the men who are sent to work single-handed in predominantly Roman Catholic, Greek Orthodox, and Mohammedan lands.

The mission stations being frequently separated from each other by hundreds of miles, conferences, or even meetings, of the various missionaries working among the Jews very seldom, if at all, take place. The three German Societies form a certain exception, for, since 1915, they have united into a conference of the German Jewish Missionary Societies, and meet from time to time for mutual deliberation, etc.

The large number of Protestant agencies at work in Palestine among Jews, Moslems and native Christians—too numerous, be it said in parenthesis, in proportion to the population—make the periodical meeting of missionaries, teachers, etc., in conference and for religious exercises possible, and these occasional gatherings are much valued. From Persia, we have the testimony of a busy missionary that, "apart from these meetings for deepening of spiritual life in connection with the Church Missionary Society's people, we could never have survived in face of overwhelming difficulties and trials."

As to how Home Churches, or supporters of missions, could help, the reply is:

(1) By prayer and the extension of the Prayer Partner plan;
(2) By sending out only the right sort of men and of good literature;
(3) By friendly correspondence between interested parties at home and missionaries in the field; and
(4) By more frequent, and more prolonged visits to the stations by secretaries, members of Home Boards, and friends of the work generally.

XI. CO-OPERATION

Mission work, whether to Jews or heathen, enjoys official sanction and recognition in the Lutheran, as well as in many of the Presbyterian Churches. But several of them claim neither supervision over the mission workers, nor do they guarantee their salaries or pensions. This is the concern of individual members of the particular Church—the friends of missions. The other Protestant denominations carry on their mission work through the instrumentality of agencies unofficially, and but loosely, connected with them. Co-operation of Churches in mission work among the Jews does not, therefore, exist, except to a small extent between the Scottish and English Presbyterian Churches, and that between the different Societies, though it exists in theory, is frequently prevented by practical difficulties from being really effective. In London, for instance, where at least half a dozen Societies are at work, the missionaries of some of them often combine in holding open-air meetings, or unite for common prayer; but, apart from that, there is little co-operation.

In Palestine, we are told, " co-operation is more honoured in its breach than in its observance. In Jerusalem, in particular, a number of small Societies, and countless individuals, all working amongst the Jews, form a most serious hindrance to real work. If the principle of comity were really observed, some Societies would depart."

For the rest, though everybody is in favour of as much co-operation as possible, it has in many areas no significance in practice, for, apart from London, Jerusalem, and some of the big cities of America, missions do not now much overlap in most towns of the wide-flung Jewish mission field. In most of the places occupied there is but one mission agency, the places themselves are generally far apart, and there is often nobody to co-operate with.

Where missions still continue to overlap, there is palpable need of comity, though much has been done in this direction since the War.

Yearly conferences of missionaries are thought most desirable, and in places like London, Hamburg, and Jerusalem a number of them have been held in recent years. But once again, the scattered condition of so many of the places, the great distances that often separate station from station, make such gatherings expensive and difficult to realise.

Only where missions to Moslems are found working alongside those to Jews, and employ a considerable number of workers, have federal councils for the particular area been known to exist, and they have proved to be very useful in many details. Apart from these countries such councils neither exist nor are they thought to be practicable, though yearly meetings of the chief workers, followed by a conference with local Hebrew Christians, might in some places, it is suggested, be arranged for the advantage of both.

Among the important needs and wants, to be met by the Churches at home, the following are brought to their notice:—

(1) More attention should be paid to educational work.
(2) Where several missions are at work, they should agree not to divide the flock into various folds, but

all to work towards the creation of one community. The conservation of converts is the most pressing need at present, and this may, perhaps, be done with the help of the International Hebrew Christian Alliance.

(3) Where Protestant Churches are to be found in the mission area, Home Boards should allocate fields to such Societies as can work with these bodies. For instance, Church of England missions should not be where Baptists have a living Church, and *vice versa*.

(4) Existing work might be more efficient if run on co-operative lines by various Societies. New developments should be the work of all Societies combined and be financed and encouraged by co-operative funds and faith.

(5) From a number of places the cry is for more workers. "Too much has to depend on one man, who has no colleague, and no substitute in case of need," writes one missionary. "During the last thirty years," complains another, "all workers and missionaries, working among the Jews of Persia, have been, with the exception of three, natives of this country. Christendom should be able to do more!"

B.—SPECIAL PAPERS

THE JEWISH PEOPLE: THEIR TYPES

BY REV. J. I. LANDSMAN, Warsaw

THE Jewish dispersion in the world is a unique phenomenon in history. No people has ever been so widely dispersed over the whole face of the earth as the Jews have been. They are to be found in every hemisphere, and everywhere they are easily recognisable as such, having preserved throughout the ages their peculiar racial type and physiognomy. In spite of untold sufferings and persecutions they are at present more numerous than ever before. In Christian countries especially, their numbers have increased in a most remarkable way. In this paper an indication is given of diverse types found among them.

A. ASHKENAZIM

(*a*) According to statistics the bulk of the Jews is found in Eastern Europe: about 3½ million in Poland, 3 million in Soviet territories, and about 1 million in Roumania. These Jews (as well as most of the Jews in Europe and America) are Ashkenazim, descendants of those Jews who in the thirteenth and fourteenth centuries were driven out from Germany and settled in Poland, Lithuania, and White Russia. Their outstanding characteristic is that they all speak *Yiddish*, a form of German mixed with Hebrew and Slavonic words. Most of the Jews who have in the last fifty years emigrated to other countries, especially to the United States, and there formed new Jewish centres, are Ashkenazim and come from Eastern Europe.

(*b*) *Chassidim and Mithnagdim.*—In Eastern Europe the Ashkenazim are divided into Chassidim and Mithnagdim. Both parties are strictly orthodox, acknowledging the authority of the Talmud and the Oral Law based upon it. The difference between them is this: that the Chassidim practise a peculiar form of piety introduced in the eighteenth century by *Israel Ba'al Shem Tob*, commonly called BeShT, a piety marked by emotionalism, mysticism, enthusiasm, and a kind of optimism. The movement arose as a protest against the dry, sombre, and punctilious piety of Rabbinism. The latter was conspicuous by its intellectualism; the study of the Talmud was considered as the supreme religious exercise and Talmudic learning as equivalent to religion. The common people who lacked knowledge and on account of their poverty were unable to devote themselves to the study of the Talmud, were despised by the learned aristocracy and much neglected. They lived in constant fear of the Day of Judgment and were deeply conscious of their inferiority as compared with the "lamdan," the learned Jew. The Chassidim began to lay stress on prayer coming from a heart filled with love to God, and taught that joy in God was the highest virtue. No wonder that the new movement spread like fire, in spite of the bitter opposition and persecution of the *Mithnagdim*, the opponents of Chassidism.

The Chassid takes as his spiritual guide not the learned Rabbi of the community, whose chief duty it is to give decision concerning things clean or unclean, lawful or forbidden, but the *Tsaddik*, the righteous one, who is either a direct descendant from the founder of the movement or from one of his many disciples. There are many Tsaddikim in Poland with a very large following, and they have understood how to surround themselves with a cloud of mystery, so that they are considered by their followers as semi-divine persons endowed with power of performing miraculous work, influencing the Deity by their prayers, and even to change the Divine decrees. The Chassid will undertake nothing, be it secular or religious, without asking the Tsaddik for advice.

The Tsaddikim exercise a great power over the greater part of Polish Jewry. They are conservative by nature; the old, the traditional, ancient customs and superstitions are to them a vital part of religion which must never be changed. They bitterly oppose all modern movements among the Jews, even Zionism.

(*c*) "*Agudas Israel.*"—Of late both the Chassidim and Mithnagdim have united into an organisation known as "Agudas Israel," with the aim of establishing the strict rule of the Thora (Law) in every Jewish community in the world, to watch that the education of the children should be carried on in the old traditional way, and to establish Yeshiboth where men may devote themselves to the study of the Talmud. The "Agudas Israel" claims to have 21 such schools in Lithuania with 3400 students, 16 in Poland with 3000 students, and now it is building in Lublin what will be the largest Yeshiba in the world. It has many talmudical schools in Hungary with about 2500 students and in Czecho-Slovakia with about 2000 students. The " Agudas Israel " is a fighting organisation striving for supremacy in every Jewish community.

(*d*) Everywhere in Eastern Europe one meets with large numbers of modern Jews who have more or less broken away from orthodoxy. A large part of them is to be found in the ranks of *Zionism* while the rest is tending towards assimilation. At the last census in Poland about one-fourth of all Polish Jews claimed to be of Polish and three-fourths of Jewish nationality. The Assimilators demand that the Jews should discard Yiddish and adopt the language of the country. The Zionists too are opposed to Yiddish, but for another reason. Yiddish, they say, is the language of the Galuth (Exile), the true language of the Jews must therefore be Hebrew. They have formed an association called *Tarbuth* (Culture) with branches in different countries with the aim of establishing elementary and secondary (high) schools in which all subjects are taught in Hebrew.

(*e*) *The " Bund " or the Jewish Socialists.*—To the Bund belongs the greater part of the Jewish working class in Eastern Europe. The Bundists too claim their Jewish nationality, but are bitterly opposed to Zionism and its aims. They are against Hebrew being taught in communal schools, demanding that all subjects should be taught in Yiddish, the language of the Jewish masses. They are not interested in religion, the left wing of the Bund is even hostile to it.

(*f*) *The Reform Jews.*—The Reform Jews are chiefly found in Western Europe and in the United States. The birthplace of Reform Judaism is Germany, from where it spread to other countries. Nationally it stands for complete assimilation, religiously, for a Judaic Theism. It has eliminated from its Prayer Book all references to the Messiah, the return to Palestine, and has also discarded the doctrine of the Resurrection. Its influence is due to the fact that everywhere the wealthy and educated Jews belong to it. But it has no future. It is spiritually sterile. The deeper spirits among its adherents are gradually forsaking it.

B. The Sephardim and other Jewish Groups

(*a*) *The Sephardim* are the descendants of the Spanish and Portuguese Jews who were expelled from Spain in 1492 and from Portugal in 1497. About 160,000 [1] were compelled to leave the countries of their birth, and the refugees divided themselves into three streams: one reached North Africa, another the Turkish Empire, and the third Western Europe. As European Turkey at that time included the whole of the Balkan peninsula and also Hungary, the Exiles settled not only in Constantinople, but also in Rumelia, Macedonia (esp. in Salonica), Bulgaria, Bosnia, Rumania, Serbia (esp. in the capitals Sarajevo, Bucarest, and Belgrade), and lastly in Budapest, whence they reached Vienna. They also founded colonies in Asia Minor, Syria, and Palestine, especially in the large trading centres such as Smyrna, etc.

In North Africa they chiefly settled in Morocco, Algeria, Tunis, and Egypt (esp. in Cairo, Alexandria, and Fayum). From Egypt they reached Aden in South Arabia.

In Western Europe they founded important centres in France, the Netherlands (Amsterdam), Germany (Hamburg), and Italy.

The Sephardim brought with them into their new home-countries not only their riches but also their Spanish language and culture. The majority of the refugees belonged to the wealthy and educated class—to the Jewish nobility, so to say. This trait of nobility they have retained unto this day, as can be seen in such a city as Salonica, where they live *en masse*. They are distinguished from the Ashkenazim (*a*) by their language, speaking an old Spanish dialect mixed up with Hebrew and other words which is known as Ladino, but which they themselves call *giudesmo*, just as the Jews in Eastern Europe call their language Yiddish; (*b*) by their Synagogue ritual and liturgy (the last of which has also been adopted by the Chassidim); (*c*) by their more correct pronunciation of Hebrew, which has been adopted by all Christian scholars; (*d*) by their purer Semitic type; and (*e*) by their deportment, which reminds one of the *grandezza* of the old Spaniards. Though they generally live in peace with the Ashkenazim,

[1] The above number is given by J. Rabinsohn. Dr M. Ehrenpreis, in his book *The Soul of the East* (Swedish), gives their number 600,000.

they never intermarry with them, which accounts for the preservation among them of their purer Jewish type. Their strength does not lie in the creation of new values, but in the conservation of the old. They seem to be gifted with a kind of active conservatism; they are the living bearers of an old, partly vanished culture. The Sephardim in Western Europe have entirely lost their old characteristics and have adapted themselves to the respective countries in which they live.

(*b*) *The Yemenite Jews.*—A very peculiar type represent the Jews who live in Yemen, Southern Arabia, where there are still about 15,000 Jews. They differ in their appearance both from the Ashkenazim and the Sephardim. In 1898 they numbered about 60,000, but on account of oppression and persecutions from the fanatical Arabs and of famine many of them were compelled to emigrate to Aden, which is under British protection, and to the Italian colony Eritrea on the Red Sea. About thirty years ago they began to settle in Palestine and during the last years before the war about a thousand of them arrived in Palestine every year. They are hard workers; in their native land they are mostly engaged in manufacturing pottery. They are very pious, and the messianic hope occupies a prominent place in their faith.

(*c*) *The Jews in Africa and Asia* represent many and different types. While in North Africa, in the towns along the Mediterranean, there live Sephardim mixed up with Jews who lived there previous to the arrival of the first-named, there live in the interior of the African continent larger and smaller groups of Jews who have been for many centuries cut off from the greater mass of the Jewish people. In Alexandria and Cairo there are communities of the original Egyptian Jews who number about 5000. Their mother-tongue is Arabic. In the oases of the whole of North-African Sahara there are scattered many Jews among the Berber population. In the oasis Wargla there are Jews who are as dark as are the Negroes, but with distinct Jewish features. (One of them I met in the U.S.A.) In this neighbourhood are to be found the Jewish Troglodytes or Cave-dwellers, who number many thousands.[1] There are also Jews in the Sudan who lived there even before the invasion of the Mohammedan Arabs.

[1] An interesting description of them is given by S. Feisl, *Stammeskunde der Juden*, pp. 99-104.

The Jews in Central Asia, in Persia, Buchara, and in the Caucasus represent peculiar and very interesting types. Especially the Caucasian Jews are in their dress and deportment like the Circassians.

(*d*) *The Jews in Mohammedan countries compared with Jews living in Christian countries.*—In general one may say that the Jews living in Mohammedan countries stand intellectually and even morally on a lower level than those who live in Christian countries. Polygamy is still practised among the Jews in Yemen, North Africa, and Buchara, while it was, under Christian influence, abolished centuries ago among the Jews in Europe. No movements of any importance have arisen of late in their midst, neither religious or cultural, nor have they contributed anything to Jewish thought or life. They have remained stationary for centuries and in many places they have sunk to the level of their ignorant Mohammedan neighbours. The influence of Christianity, direct or indirect, on the Jews in Europe has not been slight after all. The Reform-movement was an attempt to imitate the Church in the form of worship. Even the rite of Chassidism may be due to the rite of Pietism in Germany, or, as tradition will have it, to a meeting of its founder with one of the representatives of the Moravian Brethren.

Jews of Non- or of Semi-Jewish Origin

(*a*) *The Beni Israel in Bombay* (about 15,000 in number). —It is very difficult to say with any degree of certainty how much of Jewish blood at present pervades the Beni Israel. In appearance they differ but slightly from their neighbours. If originally Jews, the Beni Israel retained very little of Jewish custom until the end of the eighteenth century, when the Sephardic ritual was introduced among them.

(*b*) *The Black Jews of Cochin* on the Malabar coast are undoubtedly the descendants of slaves bought by the white Jews and converted to Judaism. They have two synagogues of their own, but there are no Cohanim (priests) or Levites among them, so that they hire impoverished white Jews of the Tribe of Levi and of the family of Aaron on the occasions when their presence in the Synagogue is required. Their number is rather small.

(*c*) *The Falashas or Jews of Abyssinia.*—There are in

Abyssinia about 80,000 Jews called Falashas, which means Emigrants. The origin of the Falashas is rather obscure. From the fact that the Messiah is known among them by the Greek name Theodorus and the Sabbath by the Judeo-Greek "Sanbat," some have surmised that they are negroes converted in ancient times to Judaism by Greek-speaking Jews from Alexandria. They do not know Hebrew nor have they ever possessed a Hebrew book. Neither do they know anything about the Mishna or the Talmud. Their religion is based on the Pentateuch, which is known to them in the Ethiopic version. They slaughter the paschal lamb and offer other sacrifices. They also observe very carefully the distinctions betweeen "clean" and "unclean." They know nothing, however, of the distinction between meat-food and milk-food. They wash their hands and recite certain prayers before eating.

Jewish Sects

(*a*) *The Karaites.*—The sect of the Karaites was founded in Babylon in the second half of the eighth century A.D. by *Anan*, a brother of the Jewish Exilarch, the political head of all the Jews in Babylon. He broke away from the Talmud and the Rabbinic tradition and established his Judaism on the Bible only, hence the name of the sect—Karaites, from Kara, Scriptures. Anan's motto was: "Search well in the Scriptures." At first the sect had great success, Karaism being widely extended among the Jews in Egypt, Palestine, Syria, Babylonia and Persia. But then mighty opponents arose and they succeeded in bringing back large numbers of them to Rabbinic Judaism. The sect is still in existence, but it has been dwindling away as time passed on. Their stronghold at present is in the Crimea, with small communities in South Russia; then there are three or four communities in Poland, one in Cairo, and one in Palestine. It is estimated that there are about 10,000 Karaites in the world.

(*b*) *Doenmeh* (apostates).—This is the name of a sect of crypto-Jews, descendants of the followers of Shabbethai Sebi, the false Messiah, who appeared in 1666. The most of them live in Salonica, but there is also a small community of them in Adrianople. Outwardly they are Mohammedans, but secretly they observe certain Jewish rites, hence they are nick-named "Doenmeh" (heretics) by the Turks. But the members call themselves Ma'aminim (Believers), Haberim (Associates), or Ba'ale Milḥama (Warriors). There are several thousands belonging to them. Several of the young Turks, as the Grand Vizir Taalat Pasha and the minister of Finance Djavid Bey, belonged to this sect.

(c) *The Samaritans,* (d) *The Chinese Jews.*—Of the Samaritans there still is in existence a very small remnant, while the Chinese Jews are now entirely extinct.

THE JEWISH PEOPLE: THEIR NUMBER, DISTRIBUTION, AND TYPES IN NORTH AMERICA

I. Number

THERE are no official, authoritative statistics of the Jewish population of the United States. All figures are based upon estimates. A conservative estimate of the present population is 4,000,000. Davis Trietsch, the Jewish statistician, has set the figure for 1926 at 4,400,000. The various estimates which have been made from time to time, with the authorities making them, are as follows:

Year	*Authority*	*Number*
1818	Mordecai M. Noah	3,000
1824	Solomon Etting	6,000
1826	Isaac C. Hardy	16,000
1840	*The American Almanac*	15,000
1848	M. A. Beck	50,000
1880	William B. Hackenburg	230,257
1888	Isaac Markens	400,000
1898	David Salzberger	937,800
1905	*The Jewish Encyclopædia*	1,508,435
1907	*American Jewish Year Book*	1,777,185
1910	*American Jewish Year Book*	2,043,762
1914	*Bureau of Jewish Statistics*	2,933,874
1918	*Bureau of Jewish Statistics*	3,300,000
1920	*Bureau of Jewish Statistics*	3,606,000

The number of Jewish immigrants admitted into the United States during the years 1921 to 1925, inclusive, for which we have statistical data, total 282,500. This number, together with the natural increase of the Jews, if added to the estimate for 1920, would make the present Jewish population of the United States in excess of 4,000,000.

As an indication of the wide range of countries from which Jews have come to the United States, and the number from each, the following data for 1924 may be of interest:

Country	Number	Country	Number
Austria	528	Rumania	5,535
Belgium	251	Russia	10,268
Bulgaria	30	Spain	8
Czecho-Slovakia	886	Sweden	32
Denmark	25	Switzerland	51
Esthonia	74	Turkey in Europe	269
Finland	7	Other European countries	17
France	432	China	217
Germany	1,980	Japan	25
Great Britain and Ireland	1,478	India	1
Greece	86	Syria, Palestine, Iraq	1,298
Hungary	903	Turkey in Asia	882
Italy	32	Other Asiatic countries	25
Jugo-Slavia	83	Africa	109
Latvia	881	Australia and New Zealand	10
Lithuania	876	Canada and Newfoundland	7,421
Netherlands	71	Central America	3
Norway	24	Mexico	316
Poland	12,185	South America	2,002
Portugal	14	West Indies	638

The Dominion of Canada

In Canada the government census takes account of persons of Hebrew origin. The figures given herewith are official for the years indicated:

Year	Number
1901	16,131
1911	75,681
1921	126,196

II. Distribution

One of the most interesting facts about Jewish life in the United States is the wide distribution of the people. They are everywhere, scattered over every state and territory. They are found not only in the large cities, but in the smaller as well. There is scarcely a town anywhere in the United States that has not at least one Jewish family. There are, moreover, 75,000 Jews scattered over many states engaged in agricultural pursuits. The Bureau of Jewish Social Research estimates the Jewish population for 1920 in each state and territory of the Union as follows:

State	Number	State	Number
Alabama	11,150	Connecticut	71,870
Alaska	500	Delaware	4,010
Arizona	1,150	District of Columbia	10,950
Arkansas	5,150	Florida	6,940
California	71,400	Georgia	23,240
Colorado	15,380	Hawaiian Islands	150

Idaho	1,160	North Carolina	5,140
Illinois	257,600	North Dakota	1,590
Indiana	26,780	Ohio	177,690
Iowa	16,230	Oklahoma	5,490
Kansas	9,590	Oregon	18,260
Kentucky	13,620	Pennsylvania	370,740
Louisiana	13,020	Philippine Islands	500
Maine	7,590	Porto Rico	200
Maryland	65,330	Rhode Island	21,450
Massachusetts	199,300	South Carolina	5,060
Michigan	71,360	South Dakota	1,310
Minnesota	33,550	Tennessee	14,390
Mississippi	3,990	Texas	32,660
Missouri	82,570	Utah	3,940
Montana	2,520	Vermont	2,260
Nebraska	14,020	Virgin Islands	70
Nevada	510	Virginia	16,020
New Hampshire	3,370	Washington	10,030
New Jersey	163,180	West Virginia	5,440
New Mexico	880	Wisconsin	30,100
New York	1,701,260	Wyoming	560

During the six years which have elapsed since these estimates were made a considerable increase of Jewish population has been noted in those states which rank high in commerce and industry, particularly New York, Pennsylvania, Illinois, Michigan, Ohio, New Jersey, and Massachusetts. The following is a list of cities which according to the latest authoritative estimates have a Jewish population of 10,000 or over :

Atlanta, Ga.	10,000	Milwaukee, Wis.	20,000
Atlantic City, N.J.	11,750	Minneapolis, Minn.	15,000
Baltimore, Md.	67,500	Newark, N.J.	55,000
Bayonne, N.J.	10,000	New Haven, Conn.	20,000
Boston, Mass.	77,500	New York, N.Y.	1,750,000
Buffalo, N.Y.	18,000	Omaha, Neb.	10,337
Bridgeport, Conn.	10,000	Paterson, N.J.	15,000
Chelsea, Mass.	14,679	Providence, R.I.	16,500
Chicago, Ill.	285,000	Portland, Oreg.	10,000
Cincinnati, Ohio	23,170	Rochester, N.Y.	14,800
Cleveland, Ohio	78,996	St Louis, Mo.	40,737
Denver, Colo.	11,000	St Paul, Minn.	10,000
Detroit, Mich.	38,224	San Francisco, Calif.	26,000
Hartford, Conn.	20,567	Springfield, Mass.	10,000
Indianapolis, Ind.	10,000	Syracuse, N.Y.	10,000
Jersey City, N.J.	12,125	Washington, D.C.	13,780
Kansas City, Mo.	12,000	Philadelphia, Penna.	240,000
Los Angeles, Calif.	43,000	Pittsburgh, Penna.	42,450

According to statistics published in the *American Jewish*

Year Book, the Jewish population of New York City was in 1920 divided by Boroughs as follows :

Manhattan	657,101	Queens	86,194
Bronx	278,169	Richmond	17,168
Brooklyn	604,380		

In addition to the cities listed above, there are in the United States 128 other cities in which there is a Jewish population of from 1000 to 10,000.

This wide distribution of Jews has brought the great majority of them into American residential neighbourhoods and under the shadow of Christian churches. The Ghetto is not characteristic of Jewish life in America. Even in large cities the Jews are widely scattered. Two or three years ago a Presbyterian pastor in Philadelphia sent out a questionnaire to the 88 Presbyterian pastors of that city seeking information as to the number of Jews in their parishes. There were 62 replies. The reports from 33 churches stated that they had Jews in their communities in various proportions up to 25 per cent. In the case of 11 churches the proportion was from 25 to 50 per cent. Three churches reported from 50 to 75 per cent., and two churches over 75 per cent. Not one of the 62 churches was able to report that it had no Jews in its parish.

A similar study was made of the Presbyterian churches in the state of New Jersey, which had, according to the estimates of 1920, a Jewish population of 163,180. Exclusive of negro and foreign language congregations, there are 355 Presbyterian churches in the state. Of these 181, or over 50 per cent., reported that they had Jews in varying proportions in their neighbourhood. Of the 217 churches located in towns, villages, and rural communities, 63 reported that they had Jewish neighbours. These facts are true for many other states and for all denominations. Approximately half of the Christian churches in the United States have Jews at their door.

Dominion of Canada

The distribution of Jews in Canada is also widespread. According to the census of 1921 the Jews were distributed by provinces as follows :

Prince Edward Island	21	Manitoba	16,669
Nova Scotia	2,161	Saskatchewan	5,380
New Brunswick	1,243	Alberta	3,242
Quebec	47,977	British Columbia	1,696
Ontario	47,798	Yukon and N.-W. Territories	9

The cities of Canada having a Jewish population of 1000 or more are as follows :

Montreal	42,667	Hamilton	2,548
Toronto	34,377	Vancouver	1,248
Winnipeg	14,390	Calgary	1,233
Ottawa	2,796	Outremont	1,195

There are 29 other cities and towns with a Jewish population of from 100 to 1000. Scores of communities have Jews in smaller numbers.

III. Jewish Types

In America the Jews are not a homogeneous people. There is the greatest possible diversity among them. Coming as they do from many lands they reveal many of the characteristics of these lands of their sojourn. They differ in appearance, in culture, in religion and outlook on life. So diversified are they that only a very general classification of types is possible.

I. Geographical Types

1. *Spanish-Portuguese Jews.*—The earliest immigration to the United States was from the Sephardic group. As early as 1633 Jews from Brazil, the Atlantic Islands, and the Netherlands began to arrive. The descendants of these earliest immigrants are a highly cultured people. They occupy positions of influence, especially in the south, where the majority of them live. This group has never been large, and though constant accessions have been made to it from Europe and South America, it probably at the present time numbers no more than 25,000 people.

2. *German Jews.*—This group began to arrive after 1740, but it was not until 1840 that they came in large numbers. Between 1840 and 1880 over 200,000 German Jewish immigrants arrived in America. They scattered over the Eastern and Middle states as peddlers and small merchants. Their descendants are to-day the proprietors of large department stores and other commercial enterprises in all parts of the country.

3. *Russian and Polish Jews.*—These constitute by far the largest Jewish element in America. Between 1880 and 1926 there were admitted 2,379,507 Jews, as many as 153,748 in a single year, and most of them from Eastern

Europe. This number does not include, for the first seventeen years, Jews who entered the United States by other parts than New York, Philadelphia, and Baltimore. These Jews are employed chiefly as factory hands in the needle, tobacco, and other trades. Many of the second generation, however, through the use of American educational opportunities, are entering the professions.

4. *Others.*—In addition to the groups mentioned, Jews have come in varying numbers from other countries—Turkish and Levantine Jews from the Near East, black Jews from North Africa and Abyssinia, etc. There is also growing up a distinct type of Jew showing the effect of the new American environment. He is American in birth, citizenship, education, and ideals. This is destined to become eventually the dominant type.

II. Cultural and Related Types

There is a great diversity also among Jews with reference to their attitudes toward Judaism and Jewish culture. They may conveniently be divided as follows:

1. *Orthodox Jews.*—This is the largest group of religious or "observant" Jews. It is comprised mostly of immigrants from Eastern Europe. They seek to preserve in full measure traditional Judaism as it has been handed down, with its various modifications, through two thousand years.

2. *Reform Jews.*—This group has sought to effect a radical adjustment of Judaism to meet the demands of modern life. It denies the status of nationality to the Jew, relinquishes the hope of a future restoration to Palestine, and declares, "Washington is our Zion." That it may meet the demands of modern industrial and commercial life it abandons such integral elements of traditional Jewish civilisation as the dietary laws and the Saturday Sabbath. It calls its synagogues "temples," and eliminates from their worship much of the ancient liturgy, introduces the use of the vernacular instead of Hebrew, and such Western customs as choirs, organs, and the family pew.

3. *Conservative Jews.*—This group occupies a midway position between the Orthodox and Reform elements. It maintains in theory traditional Judaism unaltered, but in practice curtails the rigours of the traditional requirements to meet the demands of modern life, and in worship

modifies some of the long-established portions of the ancient ritual.

4. *Assimilationists.*—To this group belongs those Jews who regard Judaism as an outworn tradition, who have abandoned the distinctive practices of Jewish life, and no longer share the conception that Jews are an exclusive, privileged race. It includes converts to Christianity and to such modern cults as Christian Science, Theosophy, and Spiritualism. To it belong many of the Jewish intelligentsia, who are largely rationalists and out of sympathy with all religion. To it also we may assign those Jewish socialists who have adopted the social creed of the brotherhood of man and the new internationalism which allow no room for a Jewish separatist view of life.

5. *Nationalists.*—The most pronounced element in this group are the Zionists, who propose to preserve and develop their traditional life in a land where Jews will be in the majority and where they can set the standards of living. Zionism in America, however, is mainly theoretical and divided into many camps, each claiming to possess the true key to the Jewish problem. There is also another element in America which holds no political aspirations, but seeks to foster the Jewish national spirit through the cultivation of Hebrew and Yiddish—the development of Jewish art, music, literature, the drama, and other elements of Jewish culture.

DISTRIBUTION OF THE MISSIONARY AGENCY[1]

For a proper understanding of the distribution of the Missionary Agency indication must needs be given of the number and distribution of the Jews throughout the world. Their total may be taken at fifteen and a half millions approximately. Of that number over ten millions, or nearly two-thirds, are to be found in European lands. In America there are now certainly more than four millions, or somewhat over twenty-six per cent.; nearly three-quarters of a million are scattered throughout Asia; the numbers in Africa are below half a million; and Australasia has about twenty-five thousand.

Returns from correspondents show that among these Jews, scattered over all the Continents, about eight hundred Missionary agents are employed by Churches and Societies. Even if we allow for omissions and for unrecorded individual workers, the gross number of agents can scarcely exceed nine hundred, and although in some countries, such as North America, England, Austria and Hungary, some ministers and clergymen interest themselves more or less directly in the cause of Jewish evangelisation, their numbers are not great, and it will probably not be an under-estimate if the gross total of Christian workers among Jews is placed at one thousand.

It might be concluded that this is a fair number of workers in proportion to the total population, or when compared with the number of agents in certain other Mission Fields. But there are considerations which compel modification of such a view. First of all, the mere fact that the Jews are distributed in so many lands and not found in a compact mass in any given country marks a difference in conditions from those which generally prevail among other non-Christian peoples. Moreover, it has to be remembered that in lands where Jews reside they are not found together, but are scattered in larger or

[1] This subject, in its relation to America, is not covered by this paper, although some particulars are noted in passing.

smaller groups through the towns and villages. They are also naturally affected by their environment, are subject to the laws and customs of so many different countries, are so diverse in language, education, social status, and conditions of life generally, that there is not, even relatively, that uniformity of culture or outlook upon life among them which characterises other masses of non-Christians living in any given area. Consequently it may be said that the Jews of the world do not constitute one Mission Field, but many, and this has an important bearing upon the distribution of and the demands upon the Missionary forces. Again, it should be very specially noted that the number of workers given above includes all classes of agents, such as teachers, evangelists, nurses, colporteurs, etc., as well as the wives of appointed missionaries. Of ordained missionaries to Jews there do not seem to be many more than one hundred, and it is doubtful whether qualified medical missionaries, devoting their whole time to the work, exceed twenty. In circumstances like these we begin to see how inadequate must be the existing Jewish Missionary agency to meet the needs of the world's Jewry.

The correctness of this view is supported by further facts. For example, a conservative estimate shows that there are over 400 towns and cities in the world with Jewish populations varying from 5000 to 300,000 or more, but the total numbers of places in which there are established Missions does not seem to exceed 160, and in a considerable proportion of these there is only one individual worker. Further, when we find that Mission Stations total about 270, it is at once apparent that more than one Mission is at work in many of the occupied places. Indeed, in some of them three or more Missions are at work. Besides, some of these Missions have large staffs, showing that a large proportion of the agency is concentrated in a relatively small number of towns and cities. To give an instance or two: Hamburg seems to have at least 30 workers, and there are as many employed in Budapest; in Bucharest there are over 20, in Constantinople 15; Safad has 12, Tiberias 24, Haifa 11, and Jerusalem over 40. For present purposes the list need not be extended, but here we find over 180 agents employed in only eight of the occupied cities. The most extraordinary concentration seems to be in Palestine, which, with only 160,000 Jews, contains more Jewish missionary agents than there are in the Slav lands of Europe, where over 6,000,000 Jews have their homes.

It is not too much to say that many of the great Jewish areas lie entirely fallow. It is doubtful if more than twenty cities in Russia, Ukrainia, Poland, and the Baltic States together are occupied by Missions. Czecho-slovakia, with 360,000 Jews, has only an occasional worker; Transylvania, with a quarter of a million, has only one regular worker; Greece, Jugo-Slavia, Bulgaria, and France seem to have each only one small Mission; in Belgium and Italy there is no Christian work among Jews at all. In each of the three North African lands one city is occupied, while two cities in Egypt have Missions. In the whole of Asia, exclusive of Syria and Palestine, only two cities appear to have missionary agencies established in them, and the total number of workers south of the Equator scarcely exceeds half a dozen.

Without going into further detail, there seems to be sufficient evidence of overlapping in certain parts and of great deficiency in others, indicating lack of clear strategic sense on the part of Jewish Mission Boards in the distribution of the missionary agency. Two factors have, however, to be kept in mind. The one relates to the political conditions which prevailed throughout a large part of Eastern Europe in the past, when it was possible only with infinite difficulty, if at all, to establish Missions in certain areas. But such conditions are passing away. The other factor is the draw of sentiment which relates primarily to the Holy Land. It is not altogether surprising that Mission Boards should desire to have some stake in missionary activity there, but, after all, if effective mission work is to be done in Jewry, it should be self-evident that missionaries must be sent where the people are. A policy based on the real, and not merely on sentiment, is required for Israel's evangelisation. It seems, therefore, a pity that the effort has been made in recent years to establish new Missions in Palestine, while so many other parts of the world are bare—all the more so, since the Brumana Conference of 1924 reached the conclusion that the present missionary force in Syria and Palestine (apart from appointments to fill vacancies, the provision of certain specialists, and for higher education) was adequate for the area. Accordingly, in view of all the above and apart from the need of the Christian Church generally to supply more men and means for Jewish evangelisation, it is desirable that Jewish Mission Boards should restudy and remap the whole field.

A few points may be noted for discussion.

1. It is a question whether some of the Mission Boards should not evacuate certain centres, where more than one Mission is at work, and enter some of the fallow fields. In this respect the great London Society gave a noble lead, when a few years ago it withdrew from Galilee in favour of the United Free Church of Scotland and left Constantinople to the two great Scottish Presbyterian Churches. With goodwill and vision, more might be accomplished along this line.

2. More actual co-operation should be possible, at least between those who are ecclesiastically akin, but not necessarily between such only. Beginnings have been made, *e.g.*, between several Societies in educational enterprise in Jerusalem, and between the two Scottish Churches at Constantinople. There is a fine example of co-operative work in certain Colleges in India, for the maintenance and staffing of which several denominations have joined hands. What is possible there should be equally possible in Jewish Missions and prove beneficial, particularly in the provision of higher education and in medical missionary activity, although it need not be restricted to these branches of labour.

3. Spheres of work might well be more closely defined, and the area occupied by any Mission left to it. In the past, much has been done at haphazard, and all too often workers of one Board have been found following or crossing the tracks of those of other agencies. An impression of unseemly rivalry is thus created, and the effects upon Jews themselves are not the best or happiest.

4. If Jewish Mission Boards desire to open new Mission Stations, they would do well to investigate the places contemplated very closely from the strategic point of view. That is to say, Missions should be started as bases from which Jews in surrounding territory may be evangelised. And having regard to the principle of comity, no work should be undertaken at any point occupied by another agency without direct consultation and in agreement with such agency—a principle already adopted by British Jewish Mission Boards.

5. As, in all likelihood, very many of the centres with larger Jewish populations will remain for a long time to come without regularly established Missions, general effort should be made to develop itineracy. But for effective itineracy well-trained evangelists are necessary, and to help them in their work first-class literature is needed. In order to attain the best ends of the itinerant mission a much larger measure of co-operation should be initiated for the training of workers and the production of suitable literature.

6. Generally speaking, no very serious attempts seem to have been made in the past to persuade converts to stand loyally together in their own home centres; much rather do they appear to have been encouraged to wander to other countries. Hereby loss has accrued to the missionary cause. The banding together of converts in the heathen world has undoubtedly had much to do with the success and progress of work. Would it not, therefore, be well if Jewish Mission workers and their Boards set their minds to this problem and endeavour to keep converts together so that as a body these might become a real missionary force on the spot? In this connection the recently founded International Hebrew-Christian Alliance may be expected to co-operate and render efficient service.

7. In view of the fact that in many Protestant communities large numbers of Jews reside, the question may be raised whether their evangelisation should not be regarded very definitely as part of the regular work of the churches and congregations in their midst. Why should Christian congregations so often find the only outlet for their missionary instincts in sending workers to the ends of the earth when so large a non-Christian element is at their doors? To bring about what is desired in this respect, more effort should be put forth to awaken the Churches to the importance of winning the Jew and to the dangers which the growth of a non-Christian population causes for Home Mission enterprise. While endeavour has been made along the line suggested in cities like London and Glasgow, only in Canada and the United States do the Churches seem to be realising in any adequate measure their responsibility towards their non-Christian populations, but their example might well be followed elsewhere.

8. There can be little doubt that the cause of Jewish

Missions has suffered from what may be called isolation. The Jewish Mission has been too commonly regarded as something peculiar and apart, and so has not struck the mind and imagination of the Church as a whole in the way Missions to the heathen have done. Yet the cause deserves the thought and support of the whole Church. As a step to this end it may be suggested that Jewish Mission Boards should seek to link up with the general National Missionary Councils of their countries. This has already been done in the United States and in Great Britain with beneficial results, and the same might be expected if similar action were taken in other lands.

EXTENT AND DISTRIBUTION OF MISSIONARY AGENCIES IN NORTH AMERICA

THE first organised effort to give the Gospel to the Jews in America, of which we have any record, was in 1812. In that year Joseph Samuel C. F. Frey, who had been connected with the London Jews' Society, came to New York. He began at once work for the Jews, and three years later a "Society for the Evangelisation of the Jews" was formed. When application was made for a charter to the State Legislature of New York, it was refused on the ground that "the proselytising of citizens is prohibited by the Constitution." The name of the organisation was accordingly changed to the "American Society for Meliorating the Condition of the Jews," for which a charter was granted on April 14, 1820.

During the century that has elapsed since that time work for the Jews has never ceased to be carried on somewhere in the United States and in some form. But it has lacked sadly in permanency. Interest in the cause usually centred about some zealous missionary whose time was chiefly spent in securing support for his work. A list of missions to the Jews during the past hundred years would be a pathetic commentary on the attitude of the American Churches toward Jewish evangelisation. There was little evidence of any serious purpose to win the Jews, and consequently the efforts put forth were timid and fitful. During these years scores of Missions were started. They flourished for a brief period, languished, and disappeared. Of those now in existence only three or four date back thirty years.

Yet these desultory efforts were by no means devoid of value. They gave opportunity for the devoted service of some gifted and consecrated missionaries. They roused many Christians to a deep and lasting interest in the work. And through them hundreds of Jews were brought into fellowship with Christ.

Missionary Work

No thorough summary of work for the Jews, as carried on at the present time in America, has yet been made. The information furnished in this paper is based on replies to a questionnaire sent out during 1926 to every known missionary agency. In most cases the reports were fully and carefully prepared, in some cases the answers were vague and wanting in detail, while from a few agencies no response whatever could be secured, though even in these instances some information has been gathered indirectly, and included.

In the United States there are 11 denominations at work for the Jews in 31 different stations, as follows:

Denomination	Stations
Baptist, Northern	1
Baptist, Southern	1
Christian Reformed Church of North America	2
Christian and Missionary Alliance	2
Lutheran, Scandinavian	5
Lutheran, United	4
Methodist Episcopal	1
Presbyterian, U.S.	2
Presbyterian, U.S.A.	12
Presbyterian, Reformed	1
Protestant Episcopal	2

In the case of 2 Presbyterian enterprises the Southern and Northern Churches unite.

These denominations carry on work in 18 different cities, employ 104 missionaries, and expend annually $254,000.

There are also 15 independent or interdenominational agencies at work in the United States in 19 different cities. They employ 67 missionaries, and expend annually approximately $230,000.

The following is a list of cities occupied by these agencies, with the number represented in each city:

City	No.	City	No.
Baltimore, Md.	2	Omaha, Neb.	1
Brooklyn, N.Y.	4	Paterson, N.J.	1
Buffalo, N.Y.	1	Philadelphia, Pa.	5
Chicago, Ill.	8	Pittsburgh, Pa.	2
Denver, Colo.	1	Portland, Oreg.	1
Detroit, Mich.	1	St Louis, Mo.	1
Los Angeles, Calif.	4	St Paul, Minn.	1
Minneapolis, Minn.	1	San Francisco, Calif.	1
Newark, N.J.	1	Seattle, Washington	1
New Orleans, La.	1	Toledo, Ohio	1
New York, N.Y.	7	Washington, D.C.	1

In Canada 4 denominations are at work in 7 different centres, as follows:

United Church of Canada	2
Church of England in Canada	3
Christian and Missionary Alliance	1
Presbyterian	1

There are also 2 independent or interdenominational Missions.

These agencies employ 16 workers and expend annually approximately $41,000.

The following are the cities occupied, with the agencies represented in each:

Montreal	2	Toronto	4
Winnipeg	3		

Unoccupied Fields

The following is a list of 78 cities in the United States with a Jewish population of 2000 or more in which no specific work for the Jews has yet been undertaken:

Akron, Ohio	2,000	Jacksonville, Fla.	2,000
Albany, N.Y.	7,000	Jersey City, N.J.	12,500
Atlanta, Ga.	8,000	Kansas City, Kan.	3,500
Atlantic City	11,750	Kansas City, Mo.	12,000
Augusta, Ga.	2,500	Lawrence, Mass.	2,000
Bayonne, N.J.	10,000	Louisville, Ky.	9,000
Birmingham, Ala.	3,500	Lowell, Mass.	6,000
Boston, Mass.	77,500	Lynn, Mass.	7,500
Bridgeport, Conn.	12,000	Malden, Mass.	9,000
Cambridge, Mass.	8,000	M'Keesport, Pa.	3,000
Camden, N.J.	2,000	Memphis, Tenn.	7,000
Chelsea, Mass.	14,669	Milwaukee, Wis.	20,000
Cincinnati, Ohio	25,000	Mobile, Ala.	2,200
Cleveland, Ohio	100,000	Mt. Vernon, N.Y.	3,000
Columbus, Ohio	9,000	Nashville, Tenn.	3,000
Dallas, Texas	8,000	New Bedford, Mass.	3,500
Dayton, Ohio	4,000	New Britain, Conn.	2,500
Des Moines, Ia.	3,200	New Brunswick, N.J.	3,000
Duluth, Minn.	2,300	New Haven, Conn.	18,000
Elizabeth, N.J.	5,000	Newport News, Va.	2,000
Fall River, Mass.	7,500	New Rochelle, N.Y.	3,000
Fort Worth, Tex.	2,300	Norfolk, Va.	5,000
Harrisburgh, Pa.	4,000	Oakland, Calif.	5,000
Hartford, Conn.	20,567	Passaic, N.J.	6,000
Haverhill, Mass.	3,500	Perth Amboy, N.J.	5,000
Hoboken, N.J.	5,000	Portsmouth, Va.	8,000
Houston, Tex.	4,000	Providence, R.I.	15,000
Indianapolis, Ind	10,000	Revere, Mass.	6,000

Richmond, Va. . .	4,000	Springfield, Mass. .	6,000
Rochester, N.Y. . .	20,000	Syracuse, N.Y. . .	12,000
St Joseph, Mo. . .	3,300	Trenton, N.J. . .	7,000
Salt Lake City, Utah .	2,500	Troy, N.Y. . . .	3,000
San Antonio, Tex. .	3,000	Waco, Tex. . . .	5,000
Savannah, Ga. . .	5,000	Waterbury, Conn. .	6,000
Schenectady, N.Y. .	3,500	Wilkes Barre, Pa. .	3,000
Scranton, Pa. . .	7,500	Wilmington, Del. . .	3,500
Sioux City, Ia. . .	2,500	Worcester, Mass. . .	10,000
Somerville, Mass. . .	2,000	Yonkers, N.Y. . .	5,000
South Bend, La. . .	2,000	Youngston, Ohio . .	5,000

Classification

The agencies through which work for the Jews is prosecuted in America differ widely in their organisation, and even more in their methods and equipment. The 57 enterprises reported from the United States and Canada may be classified as follows :

1. *Jewish Missions.*—These institutions single out the Jews as the special objects of their effort and generally have a sign in Hebrew characters, as well as in English, indicating their purpose. The centre of their activity is a hall on a street frequented by Jews, where meetings are held regularly for the proclamation of the Gospel in Yiddish. The hall is often a store or shop, generally bare and unattractive.

The appeal of the Jewish Mission was primarily to men. But of late years work for women and children has been added, and buildings with suitable rooms have been found necessary to provide for this work which is assigned to women missionaries who also visit in the homes.

In some missions a medical missionary is employed whose special ministry removes prejudice, wins appreciation, and opens a way for the Gospel.

In connection with the work of each of these missions literature is circulated, and in the case particularly of the Chicago Hebrew Mission a large number of tracts have been published.

2. *Community Centres.*—In most Jewish neighbourhoods in America families belonging to other races are scattered among the Jews. It has been found advantageous in such circumstances to minister to the whole community and not single out the Jews from their neighbours.

In the programme of these Community Centres a wide

range of ministry is usually adopted. Clubs and classes of all kinds are conducted in addition to the usual Gospel meetings. In summer the Daily Vacation Bible School and the Summer Camp have proved effective means of reaching Jewish children and young people. The Bethany Metropolitan Camp, of Roseland, New Jersey, brought five hundred Jewish boys and girls under definite Christian instruction and influence during the summer of 1926.

In connection with some centres colporteurs are employed who visit the homes, shops, restaurants, and parks of the neighbourhood for conversation and the circulation of tracts and books.

3. *Churches.*—In every large city in America where there is a considerable Jewish population, there are churches which have a large number of Jews living in their parishes. An effort has been made by several denominations to assist churches, willing to undertake such work, by appointing missionaries to help them to reach their Jewish neighbours.

Five of the fifty-seven enterprises reported in this paper belong to this category. In Temple Church, Philadelphia, where this work was first undertaken by the Presbyterian Church, as many as 300 young people are reached every week, a number of whom receive systematic Christian instruction with the full approval of their parents.

4. *Publication of Literature.*—Several missions publish tracts and pamphlets for circulation among the Jews. The Presbyterian Church publishes tracts in Yiddish and English, and also a quarterly magazine in Yiddish entitled *The Watchman.*

There are also two Societies, one in Los Angeles and the other in New York, whose special mission is to publish literature for Jews. The Hebrew Christian Publication Society of New York has rendered a very useful service in this connection.

5. *Training Workers.*—The Moody Bible Institute, of Chicago, and the Bible Institute, of Los Angeles, have each a Jewish Department for the training of workers among the Jews. In each institution there are thirty students preparing for this work who devote part of their time, for the purpose of practical training, to missionary work under the direction of the head of the department. The National Bible School, of New York City, also conducts an important open-air work for the Jews.

In Addition

Any estimate of work for the Jews in America should also take account of several other agencies not included in the preceding statement and statistics.

1. *Parish Work.*—There are thousands of Protestant churches in the United States and Canada which have Jews in varying numbers living within the bounds of their parishes. Hundreds of these churches have sought to include the Jews in their ministry, with the result that many have been led into their membership. Some of these churches have twenty-five or more Jewish members. Any adequate programme of Jewish evangelisation for America must give this service a prominent place. Hundreds of thousands of Jews can thus be most effectively reached.

2. *Christian Science.*—This American cult has been unusually successful in reaching Jews. It is said that more than 60,000 have joined the Christian Science churches of New York City alone. In some Christian Science churches it is said that over seventy-five per cent. of the members are Jews.

3. *The Roman Catholic Church.*—For several years a special work for the Jews has been carried on by the Roman Catholic Church in America. One of the Brotherhoods in the neighbourhood of New York has devoted itself especially to work for the Jews. The Catholic Guild of Israel has enrolled many Americans in its membership. Numerous converts are claimed, and a considerable number have entered the priesthood and the sisterhoods of the Church.

JEWS IN SOVIET TERRITORIES

By Rev. S. H. Wilkinson, London

1. Origins of the Jewish Population in Russia

In some portions of Russian territory Jews were established in the remote past. They were found, *e.g.*, in Armenia and the Caucasus in the period before Christ, and in the Crimea and on the Black Sea coast in the beginning of the Christian era. Many of these moved northward at a later period. Jews were found in Poland and Lithuania in the tenth century, and of them many were immigrants from South Germany.

The partition of Poland at the close of the eighteenth century [1] transferred the vast Jewish population of the White Russian territory to Russian Rule. Thereafter the Russian Jewish population became of paramount interest, not only in respect of its numerical importance, but because of its special character. Under harsh laws and still harsher administration of them, a type of Jew was evolved peculiar to Russia. The outbreak from time to time of popular brutality tended to induce sterner orthodoxy among the Jewish population as well as a bitterer attitude towards Christianity; while, far from diminishing the number of the Jewish population, it seemed to liberate forces which increased it. A reasonable estimate of the pre-war Jewish population of Russia is six to six and a quarter millions.

2. Recent Cessions of Territory by Russia and the Relative Gain or Loss in Jewish Population to the Countries Concerned

The territory ceded by Russia to Poland comprises first of all the ten provinces of the former "Kingdom" of that name (Russian Poland) [2] with the exception of part of

[1] In three stages: 1772, 1793, and 1795.

[2] The kingdom of Poland (sometimes called Congress Poland from the fact that it was created a kingdom by the Congress of Vienna in 1815 and placed under the Czar of Russia) consisted of ten provinces, viz., Plotzk, Kalisch,

the province of Suwalki: in addition Russia recognised Polish possession of the greater part of the Government of Wilna, a small part of Minsk, all Grodno,[1] and about half of Volhynia. Thus the new Polish-Russian frontier extends from a point just south of Wirballen to points north of Grodno town, west, north, and east of Wilna town to Druja and Dzisna, and then southward to a point fifteen miles west of Minsk and keeping about thirty-five miles east of the railway line between Baranowitch and Rovno proceeds to Ostrog and due south to Podwolocysk and Husiatyn.

Russia has further ceded such territory as now falls under the rule of the new Republics of Esthonia, Latvia, and Lithuania: besides retroceding from the whole of Bessarabia,[2] which now forms part of the Rumanian kingdom.[3]

By these transfers of territory it may be estimated that the Jewish population of the new Republic of Poland approaches three millions,[4] and that the Jewish population of the three Republics of Esthonia, Latvia, and Lithuania together falls little short of 600,000, that the kingdom of Rumania has, by the acquisition of Bessarabia and territory from the Austro-Hungarian Monarchy, had a much greater increase still of her Jewish population, the total of which is now given as 834,344, and that the Jewish population still resident in Russia and Ukrainia will be about two millions, rather more than less. The Memel district, which formerly lay to the extreme north of the German Empire, is now attached to the Lithuanian Republic, but enjoys autonomous government and has a Jewish population of over 2500.

Warsaw, Lomza, Suwalki, Piotrkow, Kielce, Lublin, Radom, and Sjedlitz. The present Republic of Poland is divided, for administrative purposes, into sixteen districts, viz., Warsaw, Lodz, Kielce, Lublin, Bialystock, Wilna, Nowogrodek, Polesia, Wolhynia, Poznan, Pomorze, Krakow, Lwow, Stanislawow, Tarnopol, and Silesia.

[1] A part of the province of Grodno (north of the river Niemen) has fallen to Lithuania.

[2] The Union of Socialist Soviet Republics has not surrendered its claim to Bessarabia.

[3] Finland was united to the old Russian Empire as an autonomous Grand Duchy. It became independent by its own declaration on December 6th, 1917.

[4] The Polish Year Book (1925) gives the total population of the Polish Republic as 27,193,000, but considering that it is said to increase at a higher rate than any other country, it is probably already 28,000,000; and as Jews form 10·5 per cent. of the total population, they may reasonably be said to be nearly three millions in number.

Therefore of the Jewish population of the Russian Empire of 1914, which exceeded six millions, it may be estimated that about four millions have been transferred to other states and that when all allowances for leakage by emigration have been made, about or above two millions are left in unceded Soviet territory, chiefly in Russia and Ukrainia.

3. Russia and Ukrainia

That part of pre-war Russia which has not been ceded as the result of post-war treaties, has been constituted into the Union of Socialist Soviet Republics. The formation of this new order dates from the treaty of Union made by delegates at Moscow on December 22nd, 1922, by which four Republics became included in the Union, viz. :

Russia (R.S.F.S.R.),
Ukrainia (U.S.S.R.),
White Russia (W.R.S.S.R.),
The Transcaucasian Federation (T.S.F.S.R.),

and by the further inclusion in September 1924 of :

Uzbek (U.S.S.R.) and
Turcoman (T.S.S.R.).

Thus Russia and Ukrainia, though each enjoying independent local government, are mutually bound to Soviet principles and policy. It is now no longer correct to apply the term *Russia* to the whole of the remainder of pre-war Russia. The name Russia properly indicates only one member of the Union of Socialist Soviet Republics, called the R.S.F.S.R. (Russian Socialist Federal Soviet Republic) and occupying territory extending from the Polish and Latvian frontiers in Europe to the Pacific Ocean, and governed from Moscow. Ukrainia similarly is the proper term for a southern portion of old European Russia and is governed from Kharkow. The Union of the two States as regards practical affairs may perhaps be somewhat analogous to that of Prussia and Bavaria. A military and economic alliance between the two was concluded in 1920.

Still less, of course, can ceded territory be correctly spoken of as Russia, even though it may and does contain large Russian-speaking populations. Esthonia, Latvia,

Lithuania, Poland, and Rumania, though each possessing territory and governing populations which were formerly part of the old Russian Empire,[1] can only be correctly described under their respective names.

4. The Effects of Soviet Rule and General Jewish Conditions

The information at our disposal goes to show that conditions vary very much in different districts of the Union of Socialist Soviet Republics, doubtless according to the temper of the local administrative bodies. But as the fundamental principles of government are expressed in the legislative enactments of the Supreme Authority, the Congress of Soviets, it follows that local variations in administration have nothing permanent about them. A tolerant local administration producing in its particular district conditions of comparative security and prosperity may be changed in personel or attitude and the conditions of life may become intolerable.

Of the six constituent republics of the Union, the Russian (R.S.F.S.R.) is seen to be very much the largest in extent and population.[2] It is the constitutional model for the other states of the Union. It has abolished private property in land, mines, waters, factories, and railways, and the franchise is enjoyed irrespective of religion or sex by all citizens over eighteen years of age who earn their livelihood by productive labour or who are soldiers or sailors in the Red Army and Navy.

Thus the position of Jews on Soviet territory is radically different from what it was in the old Russian Empire. Yet this fact is to be noted : true though it be that there is no longer political distinction between Jew and non-Jew : true though it be that many Jews by their superior ability and strong communistic principles have secured places of power in the Soviet administration : true though it be that there are districts where Soviet rule is mildly applied and where the burdens of life have been lightened

[1] Pre-war Russia had a population of 182 millions : the Soviet Republics have a present population of 132 millions.

[2] The R.S.F.S.R. or Russian member of the U.S.S.R. occupies 7,597,638 square miles and has a population of nearly ninety-seven millions. It contains ten autonomous sub-Republics and thirteen autonomous regions. Ukrainia has a population of nearly twenty-eight millions. No other of the six constituent Republics has a population of more than six millions.

rather than intensified, it is apparently true also that from time to time fresh waves of anti-semitic sentiment become felt in such a manner as to suggest that the danger of further anti-Jewish excesses has not been wholly eliminated.

Though the Soviet Government has disestablished the Church and appropriated certain categories of its property, and though it does not permit any religious instruction to be given in schools or classes to young people under eighteen years of age, its general attitude towards matters of creed and conscience cannot be measured by these acts. It goes far beyond. It is in my estimate unsympathetic with religious sentiment and definitely anti-Christian. True, religious or other bodies with a minimum membership of fifty may obtain community rights after the formalities have been complied with and their claims established; but *ipso facto* aggressive evangelistic ministry has no liberty at all left to it.

Nevertheless, and inevitably, certain religious movements, among Jews as among others, have been provoked into existence and vigour by the spirit of repression around them. It would appear that one effect of a communistic anti-religious atmosphere has been to stiffen the backs of a considerable number of the orthodox Jewish population, and to make them even more "zealous of the law."[1] Such are the die-hards with the spirit of the ancient Maccabees. The more prominent and widespread tendency is, however, as would be expected, towards the abandonment of all religious ritual and restraint and the surrender to varying degrees and types of rationalism, materialism, and atheism.

These generalisations cover wide but not the whole ground. It is to be noted that there are in certain localities of Soviet Russia and Ukrainia and countries adjacent, groups of Jews who manifest a spirit of independent enquiry into Christian truth. There are indications that within these localities and groups there are those, whose enquiry and desire are not merely that of philosophic interest, but of genuine soul-hunger; signs, indeed, which point to a definite movement of the Holy Spirit of God and the operation of awakening grace. This new feature is by no means general; it is purely local and exceptional. But even when the fact of its relative

[1] In 1925 the number of Jewish orthodox communities doubled itself.

insignificance is fully recognised, it remains a phenomenon of the deepest interest to all concerned for the furtherance of the Gospel among the Jews.

5. Missions to Jews in Soviet Territory

Here there is little to be said. The work of Christian testimony to Jews, which was carried on within the old Russian Empire by various organisations, now finds itself for the most part in those districts which have become detached from old Russia and which belong to other States. And these do not come within our present purview.

Of the work of the Mildmay Mission to the Jews, however, two stations were so placed as not to be transferred to other countries: they are both now located in Soviet Ukrainia, one at Ekaterinoslav on the Dnieper, the other at Odessa on the Black Sea.[1] These, with a staff of three missionary workers at each, have been and are at the date of writing still vigorously maintained, although with curtailments and adaptations to the new order of things.

Not one part of the work of the London Society for promoting Christianity amongst the Jews remains on Soviet territory, nor any of the British Society for the propagation of the Gospel among the Jews, nor of any other British Missionary organisation.

Two recently formed American organisations have addressed themselves to the task of evangelising Jews in Soviet territory, and have made preliminary journeys. We know them to have visited and ministered to existing Hebrew Christian communities; but so far we do not know of any definite evangelistic work founded or maintained by them.

It is to be hoped that agents of the Russian Missionary Society do not exclude Jews from their evangelistic efforts; but this, if so, would only apply to the attachés of the said Society who have never left Russian territory and whom the Russian Missionary Society has attached to itself by correspondence, since, so far as we know, no missionary of the Society sent out from this country or America has till now crossed into Soviet territory for permanent work.

[1] When Russia broke up in Revolution a third M.M.J. station was left operative in Soviet Ukrainia, viz., at Kieff. But that was closed in 1922, though a Hebrew Christian community survives. The work in Ekaterinoslav may also require to be terminated.

"Strengthen the things that remain." The existence of so large and needy an area of Jewish life, so closely sealed against aggressive missionary effort, may well occupy the attention of every Jewish Missionary Conference and form the burden of prayer in every heart concerned for the Israel race.

6. Local Signs of Spiritual Awakening and Enquiry

This section presents the data that we possess to justify our statement in Section 4 that there are signs in certain localities of Soviet territory which indicate a movement of spiritual awakening among Jews.

1. Mr G. Gubermann, a missionary of the Mildmay Mission to the Jews quartered in Ekaterinoslav, while undertaking an evangelistic journey in South-East Ukrainia on the shores of the Sea of Azov in 1924, wrote: "The old-time Jewish attitude to Jesus Christ and His doctrine is undergoing a change. Their hatred towards Him is completely disappearing and their love for the Gospel is on the increase."

2. The same wrote in 1925: "The evangelistic movement among Jews in Ukrainia is far greater than that we see in small assemblies."

3. Mr J. Göhring, missionary of the Mildmay Mission to the Jews quartered in Odessa, described in 1925 certain applications which had come in from groups of Jews in neighbouring towns for missionaries to be sent. When the said applications had been responded to, he described the reception of the missionaries as quite new, some Jews being apparently ready to receive Christ "at the first impulse."

4. In Odessa itself the same wrote of the attendants at the Mission Chapel as a "God-seeking people" and of "awakening everywhere." (1925.)

5. Mr Wilkinson, Hon. Director of the Mildmay Mission to the Jews, stated in 1925: "There is something almost tragic in news that comes from the country, all but outlawed from the comity of nations and where the conditions of life and liberty are so trying. And yet we get news regularly from the two centres of ministry of the M. M. J., still left behind the Soviet frontiers: and it is of a character indicating a wider and fuller acceptance of Gospel truth among Jews than we have often, if ever, known. We refrain from calling it a 'movement,' but the remark-

able receptivity of numbers of Jews to the message of the Gospel is a phenomenon to be carefully and prayerfully watched."

6. In Chisinau, Rumania (formerly Kischineff in the Government of Bessarabia, Russia), not actually within but contiguous to Soviet territory and dealing with a population till recently Russian Nationals, Mr Wilkinson bore witness in 1925 that the work of the Mildmay Mission to the Jews, superintended by Mr L. Averbuch, had influenced the whole Jewish community of the town. The same conditions of overcrowded gatherings and frequent conversions were present in 1926.

7. Of that part of the former Russian Government of Wolhynia, which has become Polish and lies contiguous to the Soviet frontier and deals with a population whose nationality till recently was Russian, an independent traveller writes in 1926 : " Jews show the greatest interest and entire lack of prejudice when the Gospel is preached. Often more than 50 per cent. of the audiences gathered was Jewish and the demands for literature were much greater than the supplies. They would stand for hours in the stuffy atmosphere and listen intently."

PRESENT DAY MOVEMENTS IN AMERICAN JEWRY

Every movement among the Jewries of the world is reflected in the life and thought of Jews in America. American Jewry cannot be separated from world Jewry. Happenings in Bucarest, Warsaw, and Berlin find an immediate response in New York, Montreal, and Chicago. But because of conditions peculiar to American life such movements take on New World characteristics, and new distinctive movements are brought to birth. There is probably no other Jewry through which so many currents and cross currents flow.

This is due in part to the diverse elements which make up American Jewry. The Jews are by no means a homogeneous body. They come from countries with very different historical antecedents, and they bring with them the peculiarities and traditions of these lands of their sojourn. They establish separate communities and synagogues, and have little in common beyond a few racial customs and their claim to Abraham as their pilgrim forefather.

In a certain town in the Middle West there are two hills with a road between. On one side are ranged three Jewish cemeteries and on the other four. Here on this side sleep the Russian Jews, there the Poles, and in between the Germans. Across the road a group of the ultra-orthodox are laid to rest, not far off is a cemetery of the Rumanians, near them one of the Hungarians, while in still another plot lie a mixed group who in life had no affiliation with any of the others. This will indicate the wide chasms that exist between some of the Jewish elements in America. Even a common ancestry scarce avails to bridge the gulf between a Spanish Jew, with his hidalgo pride, and a Russian Jew from the confines of the Ghetto. Two groups in New York were for months in conflict. It was only when they took their grievances to court that the discovery was made that they were all Jews.

Distinctive currents in American Jewish life have also

been induced by the pressure of the new environment. The conditions of life in Toronto or New York are very different from those of Eastern Europe. Daily contact with democratic principles, institutions of popular government, and the free life of America inevitably compel mental, social, economic, political, and religious readjustments. The old concepts of Judaism do not fit in with American ideals and traditions. Ecclesiastical fetters seem out of place in a land of freedom. So Jews slip the old moorings and yield themselves to the moving tides of life about them, accepting the situation as part of the price they must pay for liberty. Of the many movements which agitate American Jewry we select a few, not because they are peculiar to America, but because they seem to be the ones with which the Christian Church is most vitally concerned.

The Disintegration of Traditional Judaism

Parties and sects among the Jews are nothing new. Rationalism and mysticism from within and political and ecclesiastical pressure from without have through all the centuries sought to break the integrity of Rabbinical Judaism. But in spite of everything Orthodoxy has succeeded in holding its own. To-day, however, new forces are at work. Emancipation and liberal toleration have subjected the Jews to influences more dominating than any they have hitherto met. In America the very existence of Judaism is threatened. As Rabbi Mordecai M. Kaplan declares: " The truth is that Judaism is disintegrating. So rapid is the process of disintegration that unless it is stopped betimes Judaism will be past recovery." Orthodox leaders were filled with alarm, and a sort of Jewish "fundamentalist" movement has been organised to call the people back to the old ways and " the piety of the fathers." The revolt against Rabbinism is proceeding along three lines:

1. There is an attempt to adapt Judaism to the demands of modern life. The Reform and Liberal synagogues express this movement in its most pronounced form. They have abandoned most of the elements of traditional Jewish culture and have focussed upon ethical monotheism as the one essential of Judaism. Less radical are the Conservative synagogues, which in theory accept the ancient faith unimpaired, but in practice curtail in many

ways the rigors of the orthodox obligations. The tendency of these synagogues is to move farther and farther away from the Judaism of the Talmud.

2. Another movement within Judaism is towards a change of emphasis from the legal to the spiritual. There have arisen in America groups of Jewish mystics who are dissatisfied with the formalism of Orthodoxy and the cold intellectualism of Reform, who are seeking the springs which refreshed the souls of their prophets and psalmists. A group like the "Seed of Abraham" reverence Jesus as one who, like themselves, sought and found fellowship with God.

3. A third movement seeks to incorporate with Judaism elements from other faiths which appeal to Jews. Jewish Ethical Culture Clubs adopt most of the ethics of Christianity. "Jewish Science" is an attempt to bring into Judaism the healing ministry of Christian Science.

Each of these movements reveals dissatisfaction with traditional Judaism. They show the working of a ferment which threatens to burst the old wineskin.

The Democratising of Israel

While Judaism is not a hierarchial religion, yet by its very nature it puts immense power in the hands of the rabbis. The endless rules of the "Shulchan Aruch" lead to perplexities in regard to their proper observance which call for authoritative decision. The rabbi is the final court of appeal. In consequence, for centuries, in all matters affecting Jewish life, the rabbis have been the dominating influence.

But one of the results of emancipation, with its opportunities to secure a Western education, has been to bring to the front gifted laymen as the counsellors of Israel. An American Jewish "Who's Who" would show an overwhelmingly larger number of laymen than rabbis as the recognised leaders of the people. There are over one hundred national Jewish organisations in America to-day of a social, educational, and philanthrophic character which are under the control of laymen. And in the synagogues they are becoming increasingly influential, not merely in their financial oversight but in the direction of all their activities.

And what is even more noteworthy, in view of the

subordinate place assigned to them by Orthodoxy, is the larger place now given to women. In the Reform synagogues women sit with their husbands and children in the services, and a Temple Sisterhood, having educational, social and religious responsibilities, is recognised as a necessary part of their organisation. Even Orthodoxy has felt the pressure of the feminist movement. While women are not given the place in the synagogue service accorded to their husbands and sons, yet in the Hadassah, a Zionist organisation, the daughters of Judah have a share in the restoration of Palestine as the homeland of their people.

The Drift from the Synagogue

What is giving Jewish leaders most concern in America to-day is the abandonment of the synagogue by large masses of the people. By far the largest group of Jewish men and women is comprised of those who have no religious affiliations whatever. The heritage of the House of Jacob makes no appeal to them. The only tie that binds them to their people is that of race. They are religiously adrift.

Among the causes which have brought about this condition we may mention first the lure of economic opportunity. The modern Jew is frankly materialistic and gives himself without reserve to the pursuit of wealth and pleasure. Intermarriage is also a factor; the majority of such marriages mean loss to the synagogue. Isolation from their people in certain sections of the country has also been a definite cause of numbers of Jews withdrawing from the fold. Industrialism, moreover, has taken a large toll from the synagogue; the socialist doctrine of human brotherhood is out of accord with Jewish separatism. The Jewish intellectuals yield small tribute to Judaism; they are largely rationalists, and out of sympathy with all religion.

Jewish Nationalism

Zionism in America has taken many forms. It would be difficult to speak in general terms of the attitude toward it of all American Jews. Many are opposed to political Zionism, on the ground that Jews are not a nation and that the conception of Palestine becoming a Jewish state is impracticable. America is their fatherland and Washington their Zion. They are willing, however, to contribute to the Zionist cause that the oppressed of their people in other lands may have in Palestine happier conditions of existence. To them Zionism means philanthrophy.

The majority of Jews in America, however, are committed to political Zionism—the recognition of Jews as a nation, their ultimate control of Palestine so that the conditions of a Jewish life can be fully realised, with the right to claim for their nationals wherever they may live such recognition and protection as are now afforded to those of other races, as the English and Germans.

There is also in America a non-political nationalism which confines itself to the revival and maintenance of Jewish culture. It seeks to foster Jewish art, music, literature, drama, and whatever will keep alive the best traditions of the Jewish people and preserve their morale.

The Search for Spiritual Satisfaction

While there is among Jews in America a very decided drift toward materialism and irreligion, there is on the other hand many signs of a real hunger for God and a yearning of spiritual satisfaction. In their search they are bowing at many strange shrines. A group has become identified with Theosophy, New Thought has won the allegiance of others. Still more have been attracted by Spiritualism and zealously follow that " will o' the wisp." Of all the modern cults, however, Christian Science has made the largest appeal to the Jews. There are more than 60,000 of them in the Christian Science churches of New York alone. Some of the churches are reported to be fifty per cent or more Jewish.

While there has been no great turning of Jews to Christianity in America, there have been many indications of a change of attitude. There are many Jews who are reading the New Testament. An increasing number are visiting Christian churches. Those who speak over the radio bear testimony to the large number of Jews who " listen in " to their messages. A large number of Jews are coming under the spell of Jesus ; they have begun to claim Him not only as a prophet, but as the greatest prophet of their race. Workers among Jews declare that they have never known them to be so approachable.

In their search for satisfaction many Jews have been

led to Christ and into fellowship with His Church. Every missionary among the Jews in America has a list of seekers after truth, and every pastor who has taken an interest in the Jews in his parish knows how keen is the desire of many to understand the Christian way of life. It is estimated that 20,000 Jews are now in the membership of the Evangelical Churches of America. Hundreds of congregations have Jews in their membership, some of them twenty or more.

These phenomenal changes in Jewish life all indicate that the Jews have come to another crisis period in their long and eventful history. What it means to the Christian Church should not be difficult of interpretation. There is surely in the whole situation a call of God to do something really worth while to win this remarkable people to a recognition of Christ as " the glory of His people Israel."

THE QUESTION OF A HEBREW-CHRISTIAN COLONY IN PALESTINE

By The Right Rev. Rennie Mac Innes, D.D.,
Anglican Bishop of Jerusalem

Much of what is here said must, in the nature of things, be largely personal opinion or conjecture. Many or most of the factors in the situation are unknown or untested, but in attempting to reach some conclusions, due consideration is given to the few ascertainable factors.

The experience of the Jewish organisations during the past half century in creating and maintaining Jewish colonies of various types in Palestine is both proof and warning of the financial resources called for in settling families of western origin on Palestinian soil. It can be accepted as a principle that groups of families of moderate independent means, moved by no matter what degree of enthusiasm and sturdy purpose, cannot endure if they are dependent on their own physical and financial resources and their own agricultural experience.[1] The lesson was learned at an early stage in Zionist history. The cure (and even now it is a question how far the cure is a permanent one) was found in sinking large capital in unproductive expenditure for the general welfare of the colonies as a whole, and in making individual or co-operative loans. In other words, any colony, be it a group of individual farmers (such as the older Judæan colonies, or smallholders buying and selling in the main on a co-operative system, as in Nahalal or Kefar Ezekiel), or a thoroughgoing communist colony (like the Deganias), must have behind it the heavy financial backing of a Society which can, at need, lay out large sums for the initial expenditure (for land purchase, roads, and general amelioration, such as clearing and draining), for settlement, for securing the expert advice of agronomists, and for the varying demands,

[1] As against this can be set the moderate success of the German Templar colonies. The writer is ignorant of their history. But we are concerned with Jews not Germans.

always urgent, for subsidies or long and short term loans.

Naturally, with their comparatively long experience, the variety of their experiments and the large number and scope of their enterprises, the Zionist organisations have learnt or are learning how best and most economically to tide over individual crises, and they are usually able to transfer such reserves of men, money, and material as they may possess, wherever special emergencies arise. A new and separate colonising scheme, under a new and inexperienced organisation of not unlimited resources, would lack many of the advantages with which the present Zionist colonies are working; and the lack of these advantages could only be made good by a much greater expenditure in settlement and maintenance. The Zionist organisation calculates that it costs a thousand pounds to establish a family on the land. (This excludes land purchase and necessary land amelioration, which are met by the capital expenditure of Keren ha-Yesod, the Palestinian Foundation Fund.) A proposed Hebrew-Christian colony must be prepared for a greater cost per family. Given the desirable Hebrew-Christian settlers it is unlikely that a colony of fifty families could be settled on the land for less than £75,000, plus another £50,000 for the actual buying of the land. And even that cannot be relied upon as an end of the colony's material demands.

Very much to the point is the question of the attitude that would be adopted to any such scheme by the official Zionist Organisations. It might be faintly conceivable *in theory* that a group of Jewish Christians could work in co-operation with the present Zionist forces, rent Keren ha-Yesod land, have the advantage of advice from the official agronomists, and profit by the various loan-banks and co-operative buying and selling facilities. In the event of such a happy co-operation it is possible that a Hebrew-Christian colony might be a less expensive scheme. *In practice*, however, there is not the least likelihood of any such official co-operation. From the Zionist authorities themselves it is unlikely that there would be any active opposition: in the first place, it is not in their power to negative the settlement in Palestine of other than their own nominees; in the second place, they have no wish to antagonise the sympathies of any non-Jewish group; and thirdly, they would instinctively feel that a benevolent neutrality on their side would be the more seemly attitude to adopt towards a scheme which, in their belief, must inevitably be an expensive failure. But though there would be no official opposition, there would, most assuredly, be considerable popular dislike both on the part of the Palestinian Jews and of the Zionist supporters abroad, and this unpopularity (especially from Jews abroad) would serve conclusively to forbid any semblance of official Zionist moral or material assistance. This needs no argument. It cannot be assumed, even, that the Arabs of Palestine would extend to Hebrew Christians any more favourable reception than they have extended to the Jews themselves. The Moslem majority would certainly object to the Jewish exploitation of Palestine even if the Jews were Christian Jews.

But though the material implications of a Hebrew-Christian colony may be known or be easily ascertainable, it is quite the reverse when we come to consider the personal factors which are of vital importance both in laying the foundations of such a colony and in securing its permanence. The ideal of a colony of Jews in Palestine, all of them Christians, a permanent witness to their unconverted brethren, and a pledge of a Holy Land wholly redeemed—such an ideal has its attractions. But, granted that the great preliminary financial problems prove soluble, the question arises: Does there now exist in Palestine or out of it a body of Hebrew Christians competent and willing to make such a colony a reality? A series of awkward problems arises at once.

It goes without saying that, with such a Hebrew-Christian colony, the one impetus and *raison d'être* must be the living of a blameless Christian life in a conspicuous position. The centre of their lives must be the colony church and their common devotions. This assumes the existence of a commonly accepted body of doctrine and a system of ecclesiastical organisation suited to the special conditions of a body of Hebrew Christians. The general subject of a "Hebrew-Christian Church" does not come within the scope of this article; but clearly a Hebrew-Christian colony can never come into being until there exists a body or group of Hebrew Christians with a definable minimum of faith and practice and Church government. Does such a recognisable group exist? Small scale experiments have been tried in Palestine and elsewhere, with or without the cognizance of some patron branch of the Church. Has any succeeded? Has any leader appeared? Has any group survived a generation? Has any group, however small, propounded such a combination of Christian belief and Jewish practice as commended itself to any other group? [1]

At present in Palestine there is no organised body or group of Hebrew Christians competent to man such a Hebrew-Christian colony. If outside of Palestine there does exist such a group, there is nothing to hinder their settlement in Palestine, if they so wish, except the obstacle of expense. But then arises the second awkward problem, that of control. The colony would require financial support and, almost certainly, call for some measure of supervision in matters of religious faith and practice. Efficient control by some individual or society not in Palestine is impracticable. If the colony were controlled, and, in consequence, inspired by some individual or society in Palestine, it would probably meet with opposition from all the other missionary societies or free-lance missionaries in the country who had no share in shaping it.

In short, it is premature to discuss the possibility of establishing a colony until we have faced and solved the more difficult problem of who shall be in control of the Colony Church. We cannot conceive the possibility of any group of Hebrew Christians being endowed by their supporters with unlimited and ecclesiastical freedom. Therefore, with what branch of the Church would the Hebrew-Christian colony be in Communion? Or what type of service would be conducted there? Our only data at present show that there is almost no hope whatever that the numerous and variegated societies, and the even more numerous irresponsible individual missionaries in Palestine, can ever combine in the establishment of "one only Hebrew Church." And we dare not lend support to any scheme which will set up branches of the Hebrew-Christian Church as numerous and variegated as all the rest of the Church combined.

It cannot truly be said that there is yet any demand for a Hebrew-Christian colony. Further evidence is required

[1] To give one example only; it is difficult for those who have not lived in Palestine to realise the bitterness with which the question would be argued—Shall we observe as our day of rest and for public services the Jewish Sabbath or the Lord's Day?

before we can even be satisfied as to the reality of the need for one.

To sum up. The creation of a Hebrew-Christian colony in Palestine would demand an initial outlay probably beyond the capacity of all the missionary societies combined. Certainly no single society could undertake it. No group of Hebrew Christians exists such as could profitably be set up in such a colony. For practical purposes the idea cannot precede, but must follow the creation of a healthy Hebrew-Christian Church, in Palestine or abroad, which can furnish for the colony such a group of Christians as could worthily represent the Church in such a key-position as Palestine. Until such a Hebrew-Christian Church is in being, it appears to me premature to discuss the establishment of a Hebrew-Christian colony in Palestine.

. . . . . .

Let me add one very important note on this article. It has been written with strict reference to the business aspect of the scheme only—to the financial, the material, the practical aspect. Not for one moment do I hold that that is the only view of the question before us. In my belief it is pitifully true that there is at present little evidence of the existence of a Hebrew-Christian community which could wisely be established in a colony in Palestine. It is also true that the economic and practical difficulties are immense, and to our finite minds insurmountable.

And yet, who knows ? God may have more in store for us than we have either asked or thought, and if the dream is ever fulfilled—for as yet it is but a dream—we may be astonished and have the joy of praising Him for the ease with which He has brought it to pass. Many of the impossibilities of the past are now happy and settled realities, though for years they were only dreams. We have all heard with our ears and seen with our eyes what God hath wrought.

Therefore, even if it prove to be impossible for us at the present time to go forward with this project, let us continue to lift up our hearts to God the Father of all, in confident faith praying to Him to reveal His will, to show us clearly whether or no the dream is from Him and to give guidance and wisdom to those whom He may choose for the high privilege of working out His Will.

LITERATURE AS A MEANS OF WINNING JEWS TO CHRIST

By Canon A. Lukyn Williams, D.D., Cambridge

I am restricted to two thousand words, and, therefore, shall not attempt to describe our present literature (which, indeed, most readers of this paper know better than I), much less the vast literature of the second to the eighteenth centuries.

I limit myself, therefore, to the consideration of what new literature is required to-day if the Jews are to be won to Christ.

But may I make two preliminary suggestions ?

1. It would be very helpful if all who enter into personal discussions with Jews were to make notes of the arguments used on either side. No doubt many do this, for the practice is at least as old as Justin Martyr in the second century, whose *Trypho* is based on such notes (some, I suspect, never finally arranged by Justin), but many do not. The value of so doing is that in a few years there grows up a long record of real and living arguments, and if these are compared with those collected by other workers, a book of solid and permanent value may be drawn up.

2. If possible, secure a middle-aged scholar—I say middle-aged, because the young lack experience and the time for the aged is too short—who will make a scholarly comparison of Judaism and Christianity on their doctrinal side. I am not aware that this has ever been done in a fashion at all commensurate with modern scholarship. But it would be a storehouse of information from which many of our smaller publications could and would be compiled.[1]

[1] It will be understood that as practical people we have to bear in mind not only the needs of the Jews but also the possibility of production and distribution. The Committees of Societies represent their constituents, and these do not always understand Jews and Judaism. Nor are the members of Committees often chosen for their literary instincts. Hence the Societies are inclined to put missionary literature far into the background of their interest and work, and also do not readily accept for publication anything which differs from that to which they have been accustomed.

I now come to my real subject—What do Jews of to-day need ?

They need to see in all our writings Sympathy and Jesus. For, alas, with very few exceptions it is difficult to find either the one or the other in our literature present and past.

I. The Writers of our Missionary Literature must show Sympathy

By Sympathy I do not mean, as I need hardly say, sentimental phraseology, the pretentious affectation of emotional "gush." I mean the real and deep-seated response to the claims of Jewish learning, Jewish aspirations, Jewish spirituality. How can we expect Jews, even unlearned Jews, to care for what we say if our writings show no evidence of an understanding of Jewish literature? Oh ! I grant fully that a kind of knowledge of Jewish literature is to be found in some of the missionary literature, witness, for example, the massive learning of Raymund Martini's *Pugio Fidei*, and Paul of Burgos' *Scrutinium Scripturarum*, and even M'Caul's *Old Paths*, but as for sympathy, real sympathy with Jewish learning, even in these three books—frankly, it hardly exists.

Similarly, we must have and show Sympathy with Jewish aspirations. Zionism in some form has come to stay. We must, surely, regard it as forming part of God's call to the Jews to depart from among the Nations and be separate, and so be restored to their own land, and their true Faith.

Similarly again, we must sympathise with Jewish Spirituality. Here, I know, I am on more debatable ground, for some of our most respected missionaries do not believe in the spirituality of the present Jewish religion. I confess that I think they are utterly mistaken, for it seems to me impossible for the nation of the Jews to have survived all these centuries, supporting themselves continually, as they have confessedly done, upon their religion, if, all the time, their religion has had nothing spiritual in it. For no one, so far as I am aware, maintains that the religion of modern Jews differs materially from that of Jews of the Middle Ages or of the first centuries of our era. There is, I am convinced, an enormous amount of true spirituality in Jewish religion as taught in the

Talmud, and more especially as expressed in the Jewish Prayer Book, and other devotional literature which is to be found in Jewish homes.[1]

Let me be quite clear. I am not asking for tracts upon these subjects of Jewish Learning, Jewish Aspirations, and the Spirituality of the Jewish Religion. Possibly one or two even on these may be useful, but that is not what I am pleading for. I only want the spirit of sympathy with these to be seen in all our literature. I want every Jewish reader of every tract we issue to be able to say to himself: This author may be right or wrong, but he at least understands us and feels for us, and recognises the spiritual side of our Religion. You will never drive a Jew to Christ. If you lead him there you may be more than content. But without sympathy, plain and evident, you will fail.

II. Our Literature must show Jesus

I have read, I think, practically all our modern, and a great deal of the early and mediæval, missionary literature, and I am always impressed with this fact, that while there is in it much about the teaching of the Old Testament, and the wonderful way in which this foretells the coming and life of the Messiah, there is very little indeed about Jesus Himself. Our missionary writers have been so intrigued—to use the cant phrase—with the preparation for Jesus that they seldom tell us anything about Him as He was and is.[2]

And yet, when you come to think of it, it was not proofs from the Old Testament which won the first Jewish converts, though, of course, the Old Testament confirmed their faith. It was Jesus Himself who attracted them; His personality, His character, His graciousness, His actions, in a word, His life, and then His death, and His further Life seen of them, and known in its effect within them. We need, in fact, to reproduce Jesus. In our

[1] I may, perhaps, be allowed to refer to my article "Spiritual Elements in the Jewish Prayer Book" in the *International Review of Missions*, April 1926, pp. 205-17.

[2] "The Light of the World" by that saintly Talmudic scholar Mr Ben Zion Friedmann is a notable exception. Also I should be ungrateful not to mention Mr Loewen's *Ha Pôdeh Umatzîl*, Mr Levertoff's *The Son of Man*, and Mr Landman's *The Life of Christ*, each of which supplies something of what I desiderate.

life? Yes, above all else; but also in our words, and, that our words may go far, much further than we ourselves can possibly go, we must write and print descriptions of Jesus as He was and is. There is no harm in referring to the Old Testament and to Jewish literature as we do so. Both indeed are absolutely necessary, but they must both take a very secondary place. Jesus Himself must be our theme.

It is clear that it is not possible to put all that we know of Jesus into one tract or book. Nay, as we learn more of Him we shall re-echo the closing words of one of the earliest of tracts for Christian readers, "there are also many things which Jesus did, the which if they should be written every one, I suppose that even the world itself could not contain the books that should be written" (1 John xxi. 25). And we shall find that the longer we live, and so, by the grace of God, know Jesus better, the more we shall have to say about Him. But what sort of tracts then ought we to write? What subjects can be suggested which may best exhibit Jesus? Naturally every tract will point out His attractiveness, if not in so many words, at least in substance. For I do not see how any exhibition of Jesus can help doing that.

We need, for instance, a whole series of tracts upon Jesus as the great Example. He is the ideal Patriot (work it out in relation to Jewish aspirations!). He is keenness itself on the betterment of social relations. For, as some one has said in a different connection, "His thought of salvation was for the whole man, body, soul, and spirit." What, for instance, was Jesus' attitude to money, to the rich and to the poor, a subject very fruitful in mistakes to those who know Him superficially? I would also have a tract on Jesus and pogroms—hardly needed, some one says, and yet the very title would be a peg on which you could hang an entrancing account of the Lord's true character. Or again, one on the courage of Jesus; one on His freedom from faults of temper and speech (bearing in mind Mr Montefiore's and Mr Jacobs' attacks); one on Jesus and the use of intoxicating drink (for we have to appeal to all kinds of persons); one, in particular, on His common sense. Others will, I have no doubt, have many more subjects to suggest under this heading of Jesus as our Example.

Again, we need several new tracts upon Jesus as Saviour.

But surely, it will be said, This aspect of Jesus, at least, has not been left out! Surely it has been the aim of our Society to put the Gospel into every tract! Quite so; thank God for it. And yet, does any thinking person really suppose that the last word has been said about Jesus as Saviour? Has there not been a tendency, for instance, to insist too much on legal forms of expression to the exclusion of Jesus' character? Has the sense of His call to the poor sinner to come to Him ever been properly developed by us? Can we speak in too fresh a way of His compassion for the prodigal? Can we insist too much on His utter abandonment of all self-seeking that He might by His sacrifice make the way to His Father open to the sinner? Again, under this heading we may put new tracts upon Jesus' declarations about the use, or uselessness, of ceremonies or even good works as such, for winning salvation. Again, tracts are needed which shall describe Jesus as the teacher of the little group of His disciples, as what the Indians call the Guru, surely a very attractive subject, but quite wanting, I think, in all our literature.

Lastly, we need tracts on a subject upon which some do exist but are so very old-fashioned in style and even matter that they defeat their object—I mean tracts which tell of Jesus as the Revealer of God in His true character, and tracts which recount the personal claims made by Jesus to stand in an unique relation to His heavenly Father, and speak of His own true Deity.

No doubt it will be said that we already have tracts upon some of all these subjects. If so, so much the better. Use the old tracts as much as you like, but let us write new ones. Have you never heard Jews say that they are sick to death of our tracts—the same old things that they have had given them repeatedly? When once the Christian Church wakes up to its duty new literature must and will be provided.

No doubt it will also be said that I have omitted whole groups of subjects, *e.g.* those dealing with Jesus' relation to the Church and Sacraments. I grant it. Nor do I mind what is added if only in every tract Jesus is really put first and foremost, so that we may get out of the horrible rut of preaching doctrine and Christianity, but not Jesus.

Upon the questions of Length and Languages I have not touched. Probably if a tract is worth publishing at all it should at once be put into three or four languages. And let the length depend on the subject.

Does some one say, It is a difficult task that you have put before us ? Yes, indeed it is difficult, far more difficult than merely to equate intellectually the Old Testament with the New. For we all know Jesus so very little ourselves that we are unable to say much about Him. But if we face the task boldly we shall find that we must be much in prayer for more personal knowledge of Jesus. We shall write always very humbly, though very firmly, with a deep sense of our own unworthiness, while we cast ourselves before God in reliance on His guidance.

I doubt if anyone can do a greater work for Christ at this present moment than to write for Jews a pamphlet on some aspect of Jesus, and to write it with sympathy and respect for those who read it.

TRAINING OF MISSION WORKERS

By Rev. L. Zeckhausen, London

Some thirty years ago I happened to be one of a party that was shown round the works of a big employer of labour in the North of England, a man well known as a Christian and a philanthropist. He took the party first of all to a building where all sorts of tools were manufactured. " Gentlemen," he said, " this is the most important section of all my works, for here the tools are made wherewith engines of every description are built. Without the best tools we can give them our cleverest mechanics would achieve but little, and that is why I call this section the most important part of my works."

When asked to write a paper on Training of Mission Workers, that almost forgotten incident came back to my memory. The words of that practical and successful business man seemed to sum up in a nutshell the whole problem before us to-day—without good tools the most efficient worker can accomplish but little, whatever his sphere of work may be. It is not a point that needs to be laboured, and in theory every one will take it for granted. But are we also living up to it in reality ? At a conference of Mission workers held in the United States some years ago, an old and experienced missionary described the actual situation there as follows : " In the selection and installing of a pastor in one of our churches, what nervous anxiety is frequently displayed. What extreme caution is exercised, and how carefully the committee goes about its work. The man must be thoroughly equipped for his office. He must be upright, talented, of good repute ; he must have passed through a college or university, and have satisfied his ecclesiastical examiners. He will be, in addition, expected to be a man of some originality, an eloquent preacher, with a good figure and pleasant manners, and, above all, a Christian gentleman.

" This is for the Church at home. For Mission work, ' any old thing will do.' It is merely a question of ' sort for sort'—a reformed drunkard for drunkards, an ex-convict for the jails, a native teacher at fifty dollars a year for the Congoes, and a Jew for Jews. Let a man have the racial qualifications, let him be a Jew, and though he lack every other requisite, the Church, or Mission, is ready to commission him to preach the Gospel to his own people. Presently some evil thing crops up: mistaken doctrine, financial complications, or even a perverted moral sense, and with what inevitable result? First, the Jews are repelled rather than attracted, and Christ is dishonoured. And then Christians are discouraged, and cease to take an interest in the work."

It is a dismal picture that is here drawn for us, and one is glad to hear that things are not so bad now as they used to be. But people in a position to know assure me that there is still much room for improvement. Nor can one claim for the European Missions to the Jews that they are free from the strictures levelled against those of the States. They may be better organised and superintended, and they certainly have a longer tradition behind them, and consequently more experience to fall back upon; but of the charge of employing insufficiently educated and inadequately trained men and women they cannot be absolved either. Indeed, with the solitary exception of the excellent, but small, Institutum Delitzschianum, at Leipzig, there is not a single school or college in existence in Europe where a young man, anxious to devote himself to the work of the evangelisation of the Jews, can be at all adequately trained.

It was not always so. When the Dominican Order was founded, in 1215, in Spain, calling Christians to win the world for Christ, and when the friars decided to preach to Jews and Moslems also, they soon set aside a number of their most promising men to devote themselves to the study of Jewish and Arabic literature, and to argue with Jewish and Mohammedan scholars. And whatever we may think of the methods employed by these people, and of the use they made of their materials and position, one cannot but admire the thoroughness of their training. It is to one of their missionaries, Raymund Martini, that we owe that great collection of controversial matter the *Pugio Fidei*, which for centuries has been an arsenal that provided Christian controversialists with weapons against their Jewish opponents. And our surprise is the greater when we are assured that Raymund Martini was not a convert from Judaism, but of Gentile parentage.

And again, when Protestant Germany awakened to her duty to bring Christ to the Jews, Professor Johann Heinrich Callenberg, the founder of the first Jewish Missionary Society in the modern sense of the word, realised at once that the first and indispensable requirement was the training of suitable missionaries. The foundation of his excellent Institutum Judaicum, in connection with the University of Halle, in the year 1728, was the outcome of this conviction, and it trained some of the most devoted and zealous missionaries that ever went out to witness for Christ to the Jews. A few of the tracts issued by this Institute continue to be printed, for the use of orthodox Jews, even now by the London Society for Promoting Christianity among the Jews, which eventually became Callenberg's spiritual successor.

In its turn the London Society, though conducted on lines differing from those of Callenberg's Institute, soon found it also necessary to turn its attention to the training of workers. It began, in 1821, with a small residential seminary at Stanstead, in Sussex, placed at its disposal by the munificence of the indefatigable Lewis Way. But this was soon transferred to London, and eventually to the historic Palestine Place. Here it flourished as a missionary college from 1840 to 1895, when Palestine Place was relinquished to the municipal authorities, and no new home was provided for the Training Institution. Many were the missionaries of the London Society who passed through this college, and among them are the names of some, if not of most, of the best known of its agents.

What induced the London Jews' Society to close down its college was primarily financial considerations. The upkeep of a residential educational establishment abreast of modern requirements is necessarily expensive, however much economy be studied, unless it is liberally endowed for this purpose.

The case was very different with Callenberg's Institutum Judaicum. Theoretically his was the best, cheapest, and soundest way of training men for the Mission, but it had also its obvious limitations. Callenberg appealed exclusively to men who were reading for the ministry at the University, and offered to give them a free course of instruction in more advanced Hebrew and Rabbinics than they would ordinarily be taking, as well as in what we now call Yiddish. It did not imply much, or any, additional expense on the part either of the students or of the Institutum—it meant only the addition of a few more lectures to those young theologians. It also explains why Callenberg's missionaries were always Gentiles. His converts were generally too old, or insufficiently educated, to qualify for admission to a university and for a regular course of theology.

The college of the London Society, on the other hand, though it started with a number of Gentile students, and was never quite without these, for the most part trained young Jewish converts. This necessitated both a longer and a more diversified curriculum. Not only Hebrew and Rabbinics, not only instruction in Jewish controversy and cognate subjects, but also those ordinarily taught in a school of divinity had to be imparted here.

A question naturally suggests itself at this juncture, namely, Which of these two systems is the more practical one, the more to be preferred ? The answer will resolve itself into the alternate question, Does the Gentile Christian make a better missionary to the Jews than the convert, or is the latter to be preferred to him ?

The Institutum Judaicum of Halle had already to deal with this problem, for we read in Stephen Schultz's *Leitungen des Höchsten* that he was approached on the subject by a clergyman who urged the superiority of converts on the ground that they had a better knowledge of Hebrew and Rabbinics, and particularly of Jewish customs and habits, than most Gentiles; that they were familiar with the Jewish objections to Christianity ; were free from the age-long prejudice against the Jew that the average Gentile seemed to imbibe almost with his mother's milk; and, in addition, he thought that the Jews themselves would be more impressed by the testimony of one of their former co-religionists.

To this Schultz replies that many Jews had but a very superficial knowledge of Hebrew and Rabbinics, as well as of the Bible ; that the uneducated Jew was of little use to the Mission ; that though young Jews might with advantage to the Church be trained for the Christian ministry, as missionaries they would have nothing to recommend them above their Gentile brethren, for their mode of thinking would now be the same : further, that it was very difficult for a convert to remain impartial—he will either continue to prefer everything Jewish, and make apologies for all the faults of the Jews, or else bitterly hate and despise both the Jews and their Judaism. A Gentile can, in this respect, be more objective and impartial, says Schultz, and the Jew, who generally hates a convert with blind and unquenchable fury, will more readily enter into conversation with the Gentile missionary than with the man, for whom he has but curses and maledictions.

Much water has flowed under the bridge since that was written. The times have changed, and the Jew too has changed not a little since then. There is, fortunately, less hatred now and less aloofness. Nevertheless, one cannot deny that, on the whole, Schultz's description is not inapplicable to the conditions as they exist also to-day. The accumulated experience of more than a century's mission work among the Jews has taught us, however, that both Gentiles and Jewish converts are wanted: that they tend to supplement each other: that, if the Gentile missionary can more easily approach the Jew, the Jewish Christian can better understand him, can see things from the peculiar Jewish point of view in a way the Gentile occasionally fails to see—to say nothing of the bond that will naturally exist between him and the new believer.

In a paper contributed by Canon Lukyn Williams to the, unfortunately defunct, *Church and Synagogue*, for January 1904, this point is aptly summed up as follows: "The History of Missions to the Jews shows that these [Gentiles] as well as Jewish Christians have been greatly blessed by God for the furtherance of the Gospel among Jews, and shows also that, as in the case of all workers in His cause, the blessing given to them by God is largely dependent upon the equipment that they severally possess."

But how and where is that "equipment" to be economically obtained? Where can sound instruction in the various branches of knowledge the worker stands in need of be acquired? The Hebrew Christian educated in Rabbinism would perhaps, it is suggested, find what he required in a good theological college. This, however, is not sufficient for the Gentile or Hebrew Christian who has received an ordinary Gentile education. For these (it is further suggested) the ideal training at present would be a university course, specialising in those subjects that would be of most use to them in their work and then spend two years, not at a theological college, but at the Institutum Delitzschianum at Leipzig.

Excellent as the suggestion is, it is difficult to believe that we have yet made sufficient progress on the way of Christian reunion to think the proposition practical. Quite apart from the cost of such a course of training at home and abroad, our denominational and doctrinal differences are still in the nature of a powerful deterrent to all plans of united training of missionary workers. Churchmen look askance on Nonconformists: Presbyterians fight shy of anything savouring of Episcopalianism: and most people in the various churches of Britain are undisguisedly afraid of anything likely to be associated with Higher Criticism. But Higher Criticism is to many of them also synonymous with German scholarship, and Germany generally. It was, no doubt, considerations of this sort that made all the earlier attempts to induce British Missionary Societies to send students to the Leipzig Delitzschianum fruitless.

It is a reproach to the Churches of Great Britain that we have no training school for workers among Jews, and I personally am of the opinion that the plan, unsuccessfully mooted some thirty-five years ago, of transferring the then existing college of the London Jews' Society to Cambridge, was on right lines. The idea was, on the one hand, to throw open the lectures in Hebrew, Rabbinics, and missionary subjects at that college to undergraduates of other colleges in the university, and, on the other hand, to give its own students an opportunity for reading for a university degree. The plan, as stated, did not materialise, but it deserves to be considered again in the light of the problems that face us to-day.

I am throwing these suggestions out in the hope that they may lead to a fruitful discussion. I have deliberately abstained from discussing the Training Institution which the London Society intends to found at Warsaw, partly because the whole scheme is still in flux, but chiefly because Mr Carpenter and Mr Landsman, who are to be in charge, are with us, and will be better able to speak of it.

ANTI-SEMITISM

By Rev. J. A. C. Mackellar, Glasgow

"It is one of the strangest ironies of history," says a Jewish writer, "that the Christian Church, whose origin is due to Jews, whose spiritual impulse and highest moral lessons are derived from the lives of Jews, should have been the most implacable foe of the Jewish people and of its religious individuality." It is not, however, such a strange fact after all when it is recognised that tendencies and influences received at birth are the most dominant and lasting throughout life. Christianity was born of the conflict of old and new ideas in Judaism—the old expelled the new, the past crucified the present and future. The forces of antagonism were rampant round the cradle of the infant Church, and that spirit of antagonism between the Jew and Christianity has persisted throughout the ages until a clearer conception of the mind and spirit of Christ came to His Church and the meaning of His great word of charity, "Love your enemies," smote its conscience and a new vision of His universality cheered its spirit, deepened its faith, emptied its heart of bitter memories, and encouraged its labour of love to seek and save those who despitefully used it.

The Apostolic Church owed much to the Jew. The ideas and ideals of the apostles were cast in a Jewish mould. Their early Jewish training coloured the message they had to deliver. It was their Jewish hope that had brought many of them to Christ, but the new spirit which He inspired, the new way of life based on His teaching, the new outlook upon God and man, soon outgrew its Jewish environment. The new wine could not be contained in the old bottles. Judaism stood for the old, Christianity for the new, and between them soon raged inevitable and stern conflict. Rightly or wrongly (for the charge is hotly repudiated by many Jews to-day) the Early Church held the Jews responsible for the great Tragedy of the Cross. The part played by the Roman authorities sank into the dim background of memory. In the cry "Crucify Him" the Church recognised the shout of Jewish voices. "His blood be on us and on our children" were the self-condemning words of a criminal responsibility. "Barabbas, not Jesus" was the deluded choice that brought the judgment of heaven upon the Jewish race. So the earliest Christian preachers did not hesitate to declare, "Ye men of Israel, hear these words: Jesus of Nazareth, a man approved of God among you by miracles and wonders and signs, which God did by Him in the midst of you, as ye yourselves also know: Him, being delivered by the determinate counsel and foreknowledge of God, ye have taken, and by wicked hands have crucified and slain."

The leaders of the synagogue, the Jewish rabble of the streets strove to quench the dawning light of Christian truth by persecution and oppression. Apostles were beaten, stoned, expelled from their cities, done to death by Jewish fanatics. The challenge was thrown down. Battle-cries resounded. Wounds were inflicted that could not be easily forgiven or forgotten. Christianity was born in conflict with the Jew and that natal opposition became the post-natal disposition throughout most of the Christian centuries. The Jews' stubborn rejection of the Saviour, their calumnies and blasphemies, their blind hatred of Christ's claims and work raised a harsh spirit of hostility which kindled deeds of persecution and cruelty in hearts that had charity for all save the Jews.

The blame for the bitter antagonism of the centuries rests not only on the unforgetting and unforgiving Christian, but also on the race-proud, vengeful and boastful Jew. Judaism fosters an exclusiveness and sense of superiority which often become a most objectionable and repelling arrogance, naturally resented by the people amongst whom he lives. Each day in the synagogue it compels him to pray, "Lord, I thank Thee that thou hast not made me a Gentile." He bears himself amongst men as one who is of the chosen people and too often acts as if the world and all that is therein were somehow or other specially made and meant for him. The reward promised by his religion for piety and observance of the law is worldly prosperity, and he takes it for granted that he should have a large place in the sun—that material success should come to him, and sometimes he is not too particular in the methods he employs to gain it. So traits of character developed on this material side of his ambitions make him repugnant to many. The iron discipline to which he has been subjected through centuries of repression and oppression accentuate these features, making him shrewd if not cunning, thrifty if not niggardly, self-assertive if not unscrupulous, tenacious if not obstinate, gain-seeking if not grasping. This self-centred and self-seeking disposition, this determination to get on at all costs, does not commend him to non-Jews. His success becomes an object of envy—every step up the social ladder is regarded with jealous eye—even his abilities are only grudgingly admitted.

So the spirit of Anti-Judaism—opposition to the religion of the Jew—is reinforced by the other factors of Anti-Semitism—opposition to the Jewish race. The Jew, a Semite, with the stamp of the East upon his face and his mind, comes to the Aryan lands and the West is suspicious and distrustful of an East that dwells in its very midst. For the Jew did not assimilate. He kept aloof from the people he lived amongst—he did not intermarry or eat and drink with them. He set himself to be a stranger and a foreigner in the land in which he dwelt. He established an *imperium in imperio* in every country he inhabited. The people of these countries were conscious that there was an alien element in their midst, and there is a fundamental fact of human and animal psychology, noted by Max Nordau, "whereby every creature endowed with consciousness bears a certain animosity towards every other creature which differs from itself in appearance, habits and disposition. Especially is this the case when the differing group constitutes only a small and weak minority and we find no need for suppressing or concealing our aversion to the stranger. He can then be used as the scapegoat for all the shortcomings, mistakes and failures of the majority around him."

When the Christian Church came to power this alien opposing element was in its midst, and it forgot what it owed to the Jew in the way of blessings, but remembered what it owed to him in the way of insult, contempt and antagonism. The early fathers of the Church, Jerome and Augustine for instance, made abhorrence of the Jews an article of faith. Church councils invoked the aid of the Spirit in devising means against them. Constantine, the first Christian Emperor, urged the extermination of

Judaism as a religious duty. His son, Constantius, made intermarriage between Jew and Gentile punishable with death. In the sixth century no evidence of a Jew against a Christian was accepted in a court of law. The Jew was denied political rights and excluded from public office. He could not become an artisan because the trade guilds would not admit him. He was prohibited from entering most of the higher professions and was not allowed on the land. So many occupations being closed to him, he was forced to make the most of the few that remained open. Accordingly, he turned himself to money-lending—a practice forbidden Christians by canon and civil law—and in this sphere he soon showed remarkable financial genius. Money accumulated in the hands of the Jews and their power increased proportionately, but this financial power, often pitiless in its exactions from Christian debtors, became one of the causes of deep-seated antipathy towards them. In his lower and more sinister operations the Jew was regarded as a parasite, living not by the sweat of his brow but by the scheming of his brain—scorned, hated and feared by those who sought his aid. Increased wealth and power for the Jew only meant increased hostility and bitterness on the part of his opponents. The records of the Middle Ages are stained by frequent and fierce massacres of the Jews, by expulsions, oppressions and spoliations without number. The Crusades—that outburst of Christian chivalry—had no chivalry towards those who rejected Christ, and they left smoking synagogues and a red trail of Jewish blood behind them. The Inquisition sent countless numbers of Jewish victims to the stake. Over and over again in England and on the Continent the accusation of ritual murder was levied against them and feelings of horror and suspicion roused. Life became a daily martyrdom for thousands. Shut up within grim grey walls, surrounded by the most hampering and degrading restrictions, compelled to wear a yellow badge to declare their race and faith, they knew all the heart-breaking, morale-destroying tribulations of a persecuted people. Christendom in remembering the sins of the Jews must also remember her own unpardonable and unchristian crimes of the Middle Ages.

That great emancipating movement for faith and progress—the Reformation—brought no relief to the Jews. At first Luther was inclined to be favourable towards them, but latterly his face was set sternly against them. " Know, Dear Christian," he said, " and doubt it not that next to the Devil himself thou hast no more bitter, poisonous, violent enemy than a Jew who is set on being a Jew." This latter attitude of the great Reformer determined the attitude of the Protestant Churches for many years—the spirit of toleration was still enchained—the dawn of spiritual freedom was not yet. It was two centuries later before the political principles of the French Revolution emancipated the Jews, not in the name of religion, but of the rights of man, excluding birth, religious belief and race as tests of citizenship. In France the Jew found himself suddenly without any travail of soul, in possession of full political rights, recognised by the government of the time as a citizen of France with an acknowledged place for his religion so long as it did not interfere with his political duties.

The direct influence of the Revolution on the fortunes of Jewry outside France varied with the degree of influence exercised by the French Republic. The Netherlands, accepting from that source its humanitarian principles, gave full emancipation to the Jews in 1796 and Belgium followed along the same lines. Italy for a time reflected the spirit of France, but the return of the Princes meant the return of tyranny and oppression for the Jews and the Popes drove them back into the Ghetto, reviving the cruel methods of mediaeval Anti-Semitism. Where French influence prevailed in Germany, political freedom was extended to the Jews, but Saxony, the stronghold of German Protestantism, refused recognition. Prussia, where the overwhelming majority of Jews, especially after the partition of Poland, resided, extended through the Great Elector Frederich liberal treatment, but this at a later time was modified into a definite Anti-Semitic policy until Stein's reforms of 1812, when the Jews were given citizenship, but without political rights and without admission to the public services.

The defeat of Napoleon saw a reactionary wave sweeping many provinces and states of Europe. The Jews in many places were ordered back to the Ghetto. The growing nationalism of Germany was suspicious and distrustful of the Jew sharing in the national life, and strong Anti-Semitic prejudices arose. These, strengthened by philosophic theories, became deeply rooted in German public life and thought and Anti-Semitism became a real political force. The collapse of wild-cat speculations in the "seventies" of the last century was blamed on the Jews, and every one who had lost money through the company-promoters joined with the forces antagonistic to the Jews in the cry of Jewish exploitation and swindling. Suspicion became hatred—apathy became antipathy—objections to the Jew as a man found vent in press and on platform.

> "Die Religion ist uns einerlei;
> In der Rasse steckt die Schweinerei."

That bitter doggerel expressed the popular feeling of the time. From Germany Anti-Semitism spread to Austria-Hungary, where it was taken up by the religious parties and advocated by a powerful political party. A decade or two later it found a home in France. Although it borrowed some of its philosophical arguments from Germany it was mainly espoused by the supporters of the Roman Catholic Church and became identified with Clericalism. Its influence for a time was largely social and literary, but soon spread to other circles culminating in the famous Dreyfus case. In Russia the attitude of the government towards the Jews was marked by a capricious variability until it settled into a solid relentless hostility. Alexander I. began by measures intended to break down all distinction between Jew and Gentile. In his later years, however, that cordiality faded and was succeeded by the harsh oppression of Nicholas I., who thought it practicable to combine patronage with persecution, education with bribes to conversion. Alexander II. pursued a more liberal policy, but when Alexander III. came to the throne persecution with outbreaks of massacre and spoliation became the fixed system. The Jews were driven from the country-side and cooped up in the towns of the Pale of Settlement; all public services were barred to them and education denied. They became the poor, unpitied victims of a corrupt bureaucracy and the bloodthirsty mob.

The Great War, which forced the Jews to fight in the armies of all the belligerents, produced tremendous changes in the life and thought of Jewry. They fought side by side with many nationalities, and their exclusiveness had, for the time being, to disappear—their strict rules of dietary were broken—many of their religious observances could not be kept. Christian agencies ministered to their needs ; a new spirit of understanding and tolerance came into existence. Out of the welter of world-war came the promise of a national home for the Jewish people in Palestine and one of the age-long dreams of the Jew began to be fulfilled. The new geographical boundaries, determined by the results of the War, changed the nationality of millions of Jews. The Revolution in Russia swept away at one stroke the harsh Anti-Jewish enactments of former days and in the upsurge of the communistic wave many of the Jews rose to power. In other countries also the cause of Communism was warmly espoused by Jews, and this has served to make them an object of even greater suspicion and hostility to the conservative and privileged elements. The economic depression of the post-war years has accentuated the prosperity and worldly success of the Jew, stirring up jealousy and envy of his wealth and social position. Anti-Semitism has not decreased though its forms of expression may not be so violent. It still persists as an active and powerful force in the countries of Middle and Eastern Europe. In Rumania it has always held sway despite the provisions of the Treaty of Berlin which bound the government to grant religious freedom to all subjects, and the changes of recent years have done nothing to migitate its virulence. In Palestine, where the Jew is unfortunately tempted to be arrogant and self-assertive in the possession of his new found national home, there has been much jealousy and opposition which, however, shows signs of decreasing before his energy and industry. In Britain, where the Jew now enjoys full political freedom, Anti-Semitism exists as a social prejudice, but not as a political force or religious factor. The social prejudice is predominant in America, where also strong Anti-Semitic forces are at work.

One of the features of modern Anti-Semitism is that the Christian Church is in no way directly connected with it, except perhaps in the case of one or two countries. The Protestant Churches especially give it no countenance. It is a social, commercial and political factor, but it is not religious or ecclesiastical. The conscience of Christendom has been aroused and the Church sees the more excellent way of treating the Jew, by endeavouring to share with him the priceless treasure she possesses in the Gospel of Jesus Christ—the fulfilment of the Jew's spiritual aspirations and ideals. Within the last century missions to the Jews have been engaged in with new energy and new hopefulness, and their results and influence are beyond calculation.

The Jew is taking his place to-day in a new world of freedom; barriers have broken down and are breaking down; ideas are changing; the old is dying in the new. He is forced to mix with men of all nations, abandoning the old policy of separation and segregation, and his Judaism has to stand the test of scientific enlightenment and modern conditions. The doors of the universities in most countries stand open; the teaching of modern knowledge is in his hands; the forces of democracy are beating upon him and changes in his mental outlook and spiritual disposition are taking place. Jewry has struck its tents. The Jews are on the move. Anti-Semitism will not stop them. It will not solve their problems nor ease their difficulties. Negations accomplish little in this world. The Church of Christ must take its stand against these blind forces of prejudice and antagonism and declare openly and powerfully for the one way that will help the Jew to-day. The only way of breaking down the middle wall of partition between Jew and Gentile—the only way of destroying the enmity against the Jews as a people and as a religious sect is the way of Jesus. To that the Church has a new call in the special circumstances of our time. We have much to wipe out—let us wipe it out by our love and sincerity towards the Jew. The Jew has much to forget—let us say to him, "Forget it," and let him find a new spirit of toleration and hospitality in the Church of Jesus Christ. Learning and civilisation, democracy and universal suffrage, equality of education and opportunity will not destroy feelings of prejudice and jealousy, but the spirit of love in Christian nations and in Christian individuals will. Annihilation, Segregation, Assimilation have all failed. Anti-Semitism and Anti-Judaism have failed. Repatriation will not solve the whole problem, but the glad sharing with the Jew of the blessings partly obtained through him, the ever-ready approach to him in Christian love, and the ever-open welcome to him as one who has travelled part of the way will open up new opportunities of understanding and sympathy. Fulfilment is the word we must bring into prominence—not negation, not destruction, not opposition, not an insolent superiority, but the fulfilment of the Jewish hope and ideal in the salvation that is of the Jews, as realised in Christ.

The meeting-place is in Jesus—the Son of a Jewish home —the Christ of the Judean road, the Christ of the World's Hope—the universal Saviour. In Him alone can the feud of the centuries be ended and the reconciliation of the seemingly irreconcilable forces be secured. In Him alone can ultimate unity be gained through the power of His Cross working in love and sacrificial service till there is " no difference " between Jew and Christian, between the man of the Old Testament and the man of the New Testament " for He is our peace who has made both of us a unity and destroyed the barriers which kept us apart; in His own flesh, He put an end to the feud of the Law with its code of commands so as to make peace by the creation of a new man in Himself out of both parties so as Himself to give the death-blow to that feud by reconciling them both to God in one Body through the Cross."—(Eph. ii. 14-16, Moffatt's Translation.)

C.—DIRECTORY OF JEWISH MISSIONS

This list of Jewish Mission Organisations does not claim to be exhaustive, but the particulars given about them are as correct as can be discovered. The figures following the religious or denominational character of the Organisations denote, so far as reported, the years of origin, the approximate annual income, and the approximate number of active missionary agents employed.

I. GREAT BRITAIN AND IRELAND

Church Missions to Jews (London Society for Promoting Christianity amongst the Jews)—16 Lincoln's Inn Fields, London, W.C.2, England.

Stations: London, Liverpool, Manchester, Leeds, Birmingham, Dublin, Belfast, Rotterdam, Hamburg, Warsaw, Lwów, Bucarest, Jerusalem, Jaffa, Ispahan, Teheran, Cairo, Abyssinia, Tunis, Algiers, Mogodor.

Church of England—1809; £45,000; 200.

British Society for the Propagation of the Gospel among the Jews—9 Great James Street, Bedford Row, London, W.C.1, England.

Stations: London, Liverpool, Manchester, Leeds, Danzig, Vienna, Cracow, Haifa.

Interdenominational—1842; £10,500; 30.

Presbyterian Church of England Jewish Mission—15 Russell Square, London, W.C.1, England.

Stations: London, Cluj-Kolozsvár.

Presbyterian—1871; £1800; 4.

London City Mission—3 Bridewell Place, London, E.C.4, England.

Stations: London.

Interdenominational—1874; £800; 3.

Stations : Cologne, Frankfurt a/M.
Lutheran—1843 ; £1000 ; 4.

Evangelisch-Lutherischer Zentralverein für Mission unter Israel (Central Association of the Evangelical Lutheran Church for Missions to Israel)—Markt 2/III., Leipzig, Germany.
Stations : Leipzig, Breslau.
Lutheran—1871 ; £1000 ; 4.

V. SWITZERLAND

Verein der Freunde Israels in Basel (Basel Association of Friends of Irsael)—Sommergasse 40, Basel, Switzerland.
Stations : Basel, Lausanne, Lodz, Wilno.
Presbyterian—1830 ; £1500 ; 12.

VI. INDIA

Mission to Malabar Jews—Kottayam, Travancore, South India.

Old Church Hebrew Mission—11 Mission Row, Calcutta, India.

VII. SOUTH AFRICA

Dutch Reformed Church Jewish Mission—Johannesburg, South Africa.
Stations : Capetown, Johannesburg.

VIII. AUSTRALIA

Presbyterian Church of Victoria Jewish Mission—156 Collins Street, Melbourne, Victoria, Australia.

IX. NORTH AMERICA

Missionary Society of the Church of England in Canada—604 Jarvis Street, Toronto, Canada.
Stations : Toronto, Montreal.
Protestant Episcopal—£1500 ; 3.

United Church of Canada Home Mission Board—229 Queen Street West, Toronto 2, Ont., Canada.
Stations : Montreal, Toronto, Winnipeg, and "All People's Missions" (Community Centres) at 26 other points.

Presbyterian Church in Canada—123 Harland Smith Buildings, Toronto, Ont., Canada.

Stations : Montreal, Toronto.

Zion Society for Israel—2021 17th Avenue So., Minneapolis, Minn., U.S.A.

Stations : Minneapolis, St Paul, Chicago, Omaha, New York.

Lutheran—1878 ; £4000.

Chicago Hebrew Mission—1311 So. Kedzie Avenue, Chicago, Ill., U.S.A.

Stations : Chicago, St Louis, New Orleans.

Interdenominational—1887 ; £7000 ; 12.

American Board of Missions to Jews—27 Throop Avenue, Brooklyn, N.Y., U.S.A.

Stations : Brooklyn.

Interdenominational—1894 ; £15,000 ; 10.

New Covenant Mission—Reed and Crawford Streets, Pittsburg, Pa., U.S.A.

Stations : Pittsburg.

Interdenominational—1899 ; £5000 ; 6.

Jewish Missions of the United Lutheran Church of America—256 S. Farragut Terrace, Philadelphia, Pa., U.S.A.

Stations : Baltimore, Pittsburg, Philadelphia, Toledo.

Lutheran—1906 ; £5400 ; 7.

New York Evangelisation Society—2654 Marion Avenue, New York City, U.S.A.

Stations : New York.

Interdenominational—1908 ; £2800 ; 7.

Department of Jewish Evangelisation of the Presbyterian Church in U.S.A.—156 Fifth Avenue, New York City, U.S.A.

Stations : New York, Brooklyn, Newark, Baltimore, Chicago, Philadelphia, Washington, Los Angeles, San Francisco.

Presbyterian—1917 ; £19,000 ; 37.

American Baptist Home Mission Society—23 East 26th Street, New York City, U.S.A.

Station : Buffalo.

Baptist—1920 ; £1400 ; 1.

The Christian and Missionary Alliance—260 W. 44th Street, New York City, U.S.A.

Stations : Bronx, Chicago, Jerusalem.

Interdenominational—1921 ; £2000 ; 8.

Home Mission Board of the Southern Baptist Convention, Work among Jews — 804 Wynne-Claughton Buildings, Atlanta, Ga., U.S.A.

Church Mission to Jews—Church House, 202 South 19th Street, Philadelphia, Pa., U.S.A.

Jewish Mission Board of the Christian Reformed Church—West Sayville, Long Island, New York, U.S.A.
Stations : Chicago, Paterson (N.J.).
Presbyterian—£2500.

Jewish Mission Board of the Reformed Presbyterian Church—500 Catherine Street, Philadelphia, Pa., U.S.A.
Station : Philadelphia.
Presbyterian—£750.

Home Missions Board of the Reformed Church in the United States—Fifteenth and Race Streets, Philadelphia, Pa., U.S.A.
Presbyterian—£5500.

Home Missions Executive Committee of the Presbyterian Church in the United States—1522 Hurt Building, Atlanta, Georgia, U.S.A.

Church Mission to Jews.—Church House, 202 South 19th Street, Philadelphia, Pa., U.S.A.

Jewish Mission Board of the Christian Reformed Church.—[illegible] Sayville, Long Island, New York, U.S.A.

Stations: Chicago, Paterson (N.J.).

[illegible]

Jewish Mission Board of the Reformed Presbyterian Church.—300 Catherine Street, Philadelphia, Pa., U.S.A.

Station: Philadelphia.

[illegible]

Home Missions Board of the Reformed Church in the United States.—Fifteenth and Race Streets, Philadelphia, Pa., U.S.A.

[illegible] C500.

Home Missions Executive Committee of the Presbyterian Church in the United States.—1522 Hurt Building, Atlanta, Georgia, U.S.A.

INDEX

F

G

H

I

J

K

L